KUMON MATH WORKBOOKS

Grade **5**

Decimals & Fractions

Table of Contents

KUM◯N

Multiplication Review

Level ☆

Date / /

Name

Score /100

1 Multiply.

4 points per question

(1)
```
  9 4
×   2
```

(2)
```
  8 3
×   3
```

(3)
```
  7 2
×   4
```

(4)
```
  6 1
×   5
```

(5)
```
  5 7
×   6
```

(6)
```
  3 5
×   8
```

(7)
```
  1 2 3
×     2
```

(8)
```
  1 4 0
×     4
```

(9)
```
  5 4 6
×     5
```

(10)
```
  7 5 6
×     7
```

(11)
```
  4 0 7
×     9
```

(12)
```
  6 2 8
×     8
```

② Multiply.

4 points per question

(1)　 2 4
　　× 1 8

(5)　 7 1
　　× 5 4

(9)　 5 5
　　× 7 4

(13)　 4 9
　　 × 8 3

(2)　 3 7
　　× 2 5

(6)　 4 0
　　× 3 2

(10)　 8 7
　　 × 9 5

(3)　 5 6
　　× 1 9

(7)　 2 8
　　× 6 0

(11)　 6 8
　　 × 4 3

(4)　 6 4
　　× 2 6

(8)　 3 9
　　× 4 6

(12)　 7 3
　　 × 5 9

Do you remember your multiplication?

1 **Divide. (Use whole numbers only for the quotient and the remainder.)** 5 points per question

(1)
$3\overline{)64}$

(2)
$4\overline{)70}$

(3)
$5\overline{)72}$

(4)
$6\overline{)84}$

(5)
$7\overline{)90}$

(6)
$8\overline{)99}$

(7)
$2\overline{)178}$

(8)
$3\overline{)260}$

(9)
$5\overline{)618}$

(10)
$6\overline{)786}$

(11)
$7\overline{)990}$

(12)
$9\overline{)881}$

2 **Divide. (Use whole numbers only for the quotient and the remainder.)** 4 points per question

(1)

21)84

(5)

54)832

(9)

52)845

(2)

24)76

(6)

39)350

(10)

68)626

(3)

32)192

(7)

47)332

(4)

45)405

(8)

23)340

How well do you remember division?
Are you ready to move on?

3

Date   /   /

Name

1 Add.

4 points per question

(1) $0.5 + 0.7 =$

(2) $3.7 + 0.8 =$

(3) $5.6 + 2.5 =$

(4) $6.8 + 2.2 =$

(5) $7.4 + 3 =$

(6) $14.5 + 7.8 =$

(7) $4.56 + 8.9 =$

(8) $2.08 + 0.6 =$

(9) $0.7 + 3.62 =$

(10) $15.9 + 2.44 =$

(11) $0.85 + 4.23 =$

(12) $5.47 + 8.83 =$

2 Subtract.

(1) $2.3 - 0.5 =$

(2) $5.4 - 3.4 =$

(3) $4.1 - 2.6 =$

(4) $7 - 0.8 =$

(5) $12.2 - 2.9 =$

(6) $15.3 - 4.7 =$

(7) $6.37 - 3.8 =$

(8) $5.04 - 4.7 =$

(9) $3.7 - 1.24 =$

(10) $4.2 - 2.06 =$

(11) $3.04 - 0.79 =$

(12) $5.16 - 2.36 =$

(13) $2 - 1.52 =$

Did you put the decimal number in the right place?
Let's make sure!

Mixed Review

1 **Multiply.**

4 points per question

(1)   9 4
    ×   6

(2)   4 8
    ×   3

(3)   4 2 0
    ×   5

(4)   6 3 8
    ×   7

2 **Multiply.**

5 points per question

(1)   6 2
    × 2 5

(2)   8 7
    × 4 8

(3)   4 6
    × 7 0

(4)   3 8
    × 6 9

3 **Divide. (Use whole numbers only for the quotient and the remainder.)** 4 points per question

(1) 4)5 8

(2) 7)6 8 5

(3) 3)7 1 3

(4) 6)8 0 6

4 **Divide. (Use whole numbers only for the quotient and the remainder.)** 4 points per question

(1)

16)90

(2)

23)95

(3)

69)620

(4)

24)900

(5)

53)477

(6)

78)555

5 **Calculate.** 4 points per question

(1) $2.4+0.8=$

(2) $17.5+4.2=$

(3) $6.38+2.74=$

(4) $5.2-1.6=$

(5) $4-3.2=$

(6) $5.7-3.92=$

Nice work! Now let's check your score!

Decimals ◆×10 & 100, ÷10 & 100

5

Date   /   /

Name

Score

/100

---

1 **Multiply.**

2 points per question

Example

$0.34×10=3.4$ $0.34×100=34$

$0.342×10=3.42$ $0.342×100=34.2$

Let's check the placement of the decimal point. How many places should the decimal point move?

(1) $0.35×10=$

(2) $0.48×10=$

(3) $0.345×10=$

(4) $0.627×10=$

(5) $0.024×10=$

(6) $4.23×10=$

(7) $4.23×100=$

(8) $0.27×100=$

(9) $0.275×100=$

(10) $0.038×100=$

(11) $0.295×10=$

(12) $0.56×10=$

(13) $3.2×10=$

(14) $0.416×100=$

(15) $0.84×100=$

(16) $2.7×100=$

(17) $0.076×10=$

(18) $0.045×100=$

(19) $27.6×10=$

(20) $6.47×100=$

© Kumon Publishing Co., Ltd.

2 Divide.

Example 32÷10=3.2   32÷100=0.32

324÷10=32.4   324÷100=3.24

Let's check the placement of the decimal point again. How many places has the decimal point moved here?

(1) 43÷10=

(2) 65÷10=

(3) 435÷10=

(4) 628÷10=

(5) 3.8÷10=

(6) 38.5÷10=

(7) 38.5÷100=

(8) 46÷100=

(9) 275÷100=

(10) 5.4÷100=

(11) 394÷10=

(12) 53÷10=

(13) 3.2÷10=

(14) 426÷100=

(15) 41.8÷100=

(16) 6.4÷100=

(17) 27.3÷10=

(18) 15.9÷100=

(19) 0.86÷10=

(20) 6.47÷100=

Good job! Let's keep going.

6 Multiplication of Decimals

Level ★★

Date / /

Name

Score /100

---

1 Multiply.

2 points per question

Example 0.3×2=0.6   0.3×3=0.9   0.3×4=1.2

(1) 0.4×2=

(2) 0.4×3=

(3) 0.4×4=

(4) 0.4×6=

(5) 0.4×8=

(6) 0.4×10=   ☞ Write the answer as '4' and not '4.0.'

(7) 0.6×2=

(8) 0.6×3=

(9) 0.6×4=

(10) 0.6×7=

(11) 0.7×2=

(12) 0.7×4=

(13) 0.2×3=

(14) 0.2×8=

(15) 0.9×4=

(16) 0.9×5=

(17) 0.5×4=

(18) 0.5×7=

(19) 0.8×5=

(20) 0.8×9=

© Kumon Publishing Co., Ltd.

② Multiply.

Example $1.2 \times 2 = 2.4$ $1.2 \times 3 = 3.6$

(1) $1.2 \times 4 =$

(2) $1.2 \times 5 =$

☞ Write the answer as '6' and not '6.0.'

(3) $1.2 \times 8 =$

(4) $1.2 \times 10 =$

(5) $2.3 \times 2 =$

(6) $2.3 \times 3 =$

(7) $2.3 \times 6 =$

(8) $1.4 \times 2 =$

(9) $1.4 \times 3 =$

(10) $1.4 \times 6 =$

(11) $3.1 \times 2 =$

(12) $3.1 \times 4 =$

(13) $2.4 \times 3 =$

(14) $2.4 \times 5 =$

(15) $1.6 \times 2 =$

(16) $1.6 \times 4 =$

(17) $3.6 \times 2 =$

(18) $3.6 \times 4 =$

(19) $2.5 \times 3 =$

(20) $2.5 \times 4 =$

Are you getting the hang of it?
Well done!

1 **Multiply.**

4 points per question

Example

```
  1.4
×   3
─────
  4.2
```

① First, calculate 14×3. ⟶
```
  1 4
×   3
─────
  4 2
```

② Then place the decimal point. ⟶
```
  1.4
×   3
─────
  4.2
```

(1)
```
  1.3
×   4
```

(5)
```
  1.6
×   5
```

☞ Write the answer
as '8' and not
'8.0.'

(9)
```
  4.2
×   7
```

(13)
```
  2.8
×   9
```

(2)
```
  1.3
×   6
```

(6)
```
  2.4
×   3
```

(10)
```
  2.9
×   6
```

(3)
```
  1.3
×   8
```

(7)
```
  2.4
×   6
```

(11)
```
  0.7
×   8
```

(4)
```
  1.6
×   3
```

(8)
```
  3.6
×   4
```

(12)
```
  4.3
×   5
```

© Kumon Publishing Co., Ltd.

2 Multiply.

(1) $\begin{array}{r} 1.2 \\ \times\ \ 6 \\ \hline \end{array}$

(5) $\begin{array}{r} 0.9 \\ \times\ \ 7 \\ \hline \end{array}$

(9) $\begin{array}{r} 12.4 \\ \times\ \ \ \ 3 \\ \hline \end{array}$

(13) $\begin{array}{r} 30.7 \\ \times\ \ \ \ 8 \\ \hline \end{array}$

(2) $\begin{array}{r} 5.4 \\ \times\ \ 3 \\ \hline \end{array}$

(6) $\begin{array}{r} 7.2 \\ \times\ \ 4 \\ \hline \end{array}$

(10) $\begin{array}{r} 12.8 \\ \times\ \ \ \ 5 \\ \hline \end{array}$

(14) $\begin{array}{r} 42.5 \\ \times\ \ \ \ 6 \\ \hline \end{array}$

(3) $\begin{array}{r} 2.7 \\ \times\ \ 8 \\ \hline \end{array}$

(7) $\begin{array}{r} 5.8 \\ \times\ \ 6 \\ \hline \end{array}$

(11) $\begin{array}{r} 21.4 \\ \times\ \ \ \ 2 \\ \hline \end{array}$

(15) $\begin{array}{r} 18.2 \\ \times\ \ \ \ 8 \\ \hline \end{array}$

(4) $\begin{array}{r} 3.5 \\ \times\ \ 4 \\ \hline \end{array}$

(8) $\begin{array}{r} 4.9 \\ \times\ \ 8 \\ \hline \end{array}$

(12) $\begin{array}{r} 24.6 \\ \times\ \ \ \ 4 \\ \hline \end{array}$

(16) $\begin{array}{r} 27.4 \\ \times\ \ \ \ 9 \\ \hline \end{array}$

Let's try to pay close attention to the placement of the decimal point in your answers!

Multiplication of Decimals

Date / /

Name

Level ★★★

Score /100

---

1 **Multiply.**

4 points per question

Example

$$\begin{array}{r} 1.16 \\ \times\ \ \ \ 3 \\ \hline 3.48 \end{array}$$

① First, calculate 116 × 3. ⟶

$$\begin{array}{r} 116 \\ \times\ \ \ \ 3 \\ \hline 348 \end{array}$$

② Then place the decimal point. ⟶

$$\begin{array}{r} 1.16 \\ \times\ \ \ \ 3 \\ \hline 3.48 \end{array}$$

---

(1)
$$\begin{array}{r} 1.28 \\ \times\ \ \ \ 3 \\ \hline \end{array}$$

(5)
$$\begin{array}{r} 2.14 \\ \times\ \ \ \ 6 \\ \hline \end{array}$$

(9)
$$\begin{array}{r} 1.24 \\ \times\ \ \ \ 7 \\ \hline \end{array}$$

(13)
$$\begin{array}{r} 2.74 \\ \times\ \ \ \ 9 \\ \hline \end{array}$$

(2)
$$\begin{array}{r} 1.28 \\ \times\ \ \ \ 4 \\ \hline \end{array}$$

(6)
$$\begin{array}{r} 3.26 \\ \times\ \ \ \ 3 \\ \hline \end{array}$$

(10)
$$\begin{array}{r} 2.76 \\ \times\ \ \ \ 3 \\ \hline \end{array}$$

(3)
$$\begin{array}{r} 1.28 \\ \times\ \ \ \ 5 \\ \hline \end{array}$$

☞ Write the answer as `6.4' and not `6.40.'

(7)
$$\begin{array}{r} 3.26 \\ \times\ \ \ \ 5 \\ \hline \end{array}$$

(11)
$$\begin{array}{r} 4.23 \\ \times\ \ \ \ 4 \\ \hline \end{array}$$

(4)
$$\begin{array}{r} 2.14 \\ \times\ \ \ \ 2 \\ \hline \end{array}$$

(8)
$$\begin{array}{r} 1.63 \\ \times\ \ \ \ 2 \\ \hline \end{array}$$

(12)
$$\begin{array}{r} 3.82 \\ \times\ \ \ \ 5 \\ \hline \end{array}$$

(1)   1.2 4
    ×   3

(5)   0.6 4
    ×   6

(9)   2.4 6
    ×   4

(13)   2.0 3
    ×   8

(2)   1.2 8
    ×   5

(6)   0.3 9
    ×   5

(10)   4.0 3
    ×   5

(14)   0.4 7
    ×   6

(3)   0.7 5
    ×   3

(7)   3.0 6
    ×   7

(11)   0.9 2
    ×   6

(15)   0.0 4 7
    ×   6

(4)   2.0 7
    ×   4

(8)   1.0 8
    ×   4

(12)   3.8 4
    ×   5

(16)   0.2 3 6
    ×   4

If you made a mistake, just try the problem again.
You can do it!

Multiplication of Decimals

Date / /

Name

Score /100

1 Multiply.

4 points per question

Example

$$\begin{array}{r} 1\,6 \\ \times\,0.3 \\ \hline 4.8 \end{array}$$

① First, calculate 16×3. ⟶

$$\begin{array}{r} 1\,6 \\ \times\quad 3 \\ \hline 4\,8 \end{array}$$

② Then place the decimal point. ⟶

$$\begin{array}{r} 1\,6 \\ \times\,0.3 \\ \hline 4.8 \end{array}$$

(1)
$$\begin{array}{r} 1\,2 \\ \times\,0.7 \end{array}$$

(2)
$$\begin{array}{r} 1\,2 \\ \times\,0.8 \end{array}$$

(3)
$$\begin{array}{r} 1\,8 \\ \times\,0.7 \end{array}$$

(4)
$$\begin{array}{r} 1\,8 \\ \times\,0.9 \end{array}$$

(5)
$$\begin{array}{r} 2\,5 \\ \times\,0.7 \end{array}$$

(6)
$$\begin{array}{r} 2\,5 \\ \times\,0.4 \end{array}$$

(7)
$$\begin{array}{r} 2\,5 \\ \times\,0.9 \end{array}$$

(8)
$$\begin{array}{r} 2\,9 \\ \times\,0.4 \end{array}$$

(9)
$$\begin{array}{r} 3\,6 \\ \times\,0.4 \end{array}$$

(10)
$$\begin{array}{r} 3\,7 \\ \times\,0.4 \end{array}$$

(11)
$$\begin{array}{r} 4\,2 \\ \times\,0.7 \end{array}$$

(12)
$$\begin{array}{r} 4\,3 \\ \times\,0.5 \end{array}$$

(13)
$$\begin{array}{r} 2\,8 \\ \times\,0.9 \end{array}$$

(1)　　1 2
　　×0.6

(5)　　　9
　　×0.7

(9)　　1 2 4
　　×　0.3

(13)　　3 2 7
　　×　0.8

(2)　　5 4
　　×0.3

(6)　　7 2
　　×0.4

(10)　　1 2 8
　　×　0.6

(14)　　4 5 6
　　×　0.6

(3)　　2 6
　　×0.8

(7)　　5 6
　　×0.3

(11)　　2 3 5
　　×　0.7

(15)　　3 7 2
　　×　0.4

(4)　　3 5
　　×0.4

(8)　　4 7
　　×0.8

(12)　　2 4 6
　　×　0.4

(16)　　5 4 3
　　×　0.8

Did you solve all of the problems?
Let's check your answers.

1 **Multiply.**

5 points per question

Example

$$
\begin{array}{r}
1\,6 \\
\times 1.4 \\
\hline
6\,4 \\
1\,6 \\
\hline
2\,2.4
\end{array}
$$

(1)
$$
\begin{array}{r}
1\,6 \\
\times 1.2 \\
\hline
\end{array}
$$

(4)
$$
\begin{array}{r}
2\,3 \\
\times 1.8 \\
\hline
\end{array}
$$

(7)
$$
\begin{array}{r}
3\,8 \\
\times 2.7 \\
\hline
\end{array}
$$

(10)
$$
\begin{array}{r}
5\,2 \\
\times 2.8 \\
\hline
\end{array}
$$

(2)
$$
\begin{array}{r}
1\,6 \\
\times 2.3 \\
\hline
\end{array}
$$

(5)
$$
\begin{array}{r}
2\,3 \\
\times 2.5 \\
\hline
\end{array}
$$

(8)
$$
\begin{array}{r}
4\,2 \\
\times 1.7 \\
\hline
\end{array}
$$

(3)
$$
\begin{array}{r}
2\,3 \\
\times 1.4 \\
\hline
\end{array}
$$

(6)
$$
\begin{array}{r}
3\,4 \\
\times 1.6 \\
\hline
\end{array}
$$

(9)
$$
\begin{array}{r}
4\,6 \\
\times 2.5 \\
\hline
\end{array}
$$

② Multiply.

Example

```
    1.6
  × 1 2
  ─────
    3 2
  1 6
  ─────
  1 9.2
```

(1)
```
    1.6
  × 1 4
```

(2)
```
    1.8
  × 1 7
```

(3)
```
    2.4
  × 1 3
```

(4)
```
    1.7
  × 2 6
```

(5)
```
    1.5
  × 2 9
```

(6)
```
    1.9
  × 4 3
```

(7)
```
    3.2
  × 2 5
```

(8)
```
    3.8
  × 2 7
```

(9)
```
    4.5
  × 3 6
```

(10)
```
    5.6
  × 2 7
```

That's good. Let's practice some more!

Multiplication of Decimals

Level ★★★

Score

/100

1 Multiply.

5 points per question

Example

```
   1.36
 ×   12
   272
  136
 16.32
```

(1)
```
   1.36
 ×   14
```

(4)
```
   1.72
 ×   24
```

(7)
```
   3.15
 ×   26
```

(10)
```
   5.03
 ×   28
```

(2)
```
   1.48
 ×   13
```

(5)
```
   1.56
 ×   29
```

(8)
```
   3.06
 ×   27
```

(3)
```
   2.13
 ×   18
```

(6)
```
   1.24
 ×   46
```

(9)
```
   4.68
 ×   34
```

2 Multiply.

Example

$$\begin{array}{r} 0.6 \\ \times\ 1\ 2 \\ \hline 1\ 2 \\ 6\quad \\ \hline 7.2 \end{array}$$

(1)
$$\begin{array}{r} 0.6 \\ \times\ 1\ 4 \\ \hline \end{array}$$

(4)
$$\begin{array}{r} 0.7 \\ \times\ 2\ 6 \\ \hline \end{array}$$

(7)
$$\begin{array}{r} 0.6 \\ \times\ 2\ 8 \\ \hline \end{array}$$

(10)
$$\begin{array}{r} 0.7 \\ \times\ 4\ 6 \\ \hline \end{array}$$

(2)
$$\begin{array}{r} 0.8 \\ \times\ 1\ 7 \\ \hline \end{array}$$

(5)
$$\begin{array}{r} 0.9 \\ \times\ 1\ 5 \\ \hline \end{array}$$

(8)
$$\begin{array}{r} 0.8 \\ \times\ 3\ 2 \\ \hline \end{array}$$

(3)
$$\begin{array}{r} 0.7 \\ \times\ 1\ 4 \\ \hline \end{array}$$

(6)
$$\begin{array}{r} 0.4 \\ \times\ 2\ 3 \\ \hline \end{array}$$

(9)
$$\begin{array}{r} 0.9 \\ \times\ 3\ 4 \\ \hline \end{array}$$

Don't forget to make sure your decimal points are in the right place!

Multiplication of Decimals

Level
★★★

Date / /

Name

Score
/100

1 **Multiply.**

4 points per question

Example

```
   0.3 6
 ×   1 2
───────
   7 2
 3 6
───────
 4.3 2
```

(1)
```
   0.3 6
 ×   1 4
```

(4)
```
   0.2 5
 ×   1 4
```

(7)
```
   0.4 6
 ×   2 8
```

(10)
```
   0.5 2
 ×   2 6
```

(2)
```
   0.2 8
 ×   1 3
```

(5)
```
   0.4 3
 ×   1 5
```

(8)
```
   0.2 4
 ×   4 7
```

(3)
```
   0.3 2
 ×   1 6
```

(6)
```
   0.3 2
 ×   2 7
```

(9)
```
   0.3 9
 ×   3 2
```

② Multiply.

Example

① First, calculate 8 × 3.

② Then place the decimal point.

```
  0.8
×0.3
─────
0.2 4
```

```
   8
× 3
─────
2 4
```

```
  0.8 ── Here, the decimal point is one digit
          from the right.
×0.3 ── Here, the decimal point is also one
          digit from the right.
─────
0.2 4 ── Therefore, move this decimal point
          two digits from the right.
```

(1)
```
  0.8
×0.2
```

(2)
```
  0.8
×0.6
```

(3)
```
  0.6
×0.4
```

(4)
```
  0.6
×0.7
```

(5)
```
  0.9
×0.5
```

(6)
```
  0.9
×0.8
```

(7)
```
  0.7
×0.6
```

(8)
```
  0.7
×0.9
```

(9)
```
  0.4
×0.8
```

(10)
```
  0.4
×0.5
```

(11)
```
  0.5
×0.7
```

(12)
```
  0.5
×0.8
```

Practice makes perfect. Let's keep going!

Multiplication of Decimals

Level ★★

Date　　/　　/　　Name

Score　　　/100

1 Multiply.

4 points per question

Example

　　①First, calculate 14 × 3.　　②Then place the decimal point.

$$\begin{array}{r} 1.4 \\ \times\,0.3 \\ \hline 0.4\,2 \end{array}$$

$$\begin{array}{r} 1\,4 \\ \times\quad 3 \\ \hline 4\,2 \end{array}$$

1.4 — Here, the decimal point is one digit from the right.

×0.3 — Here, the decimal point is also one digit from the right.

0.42

Therefore, move this decimal point two digits from the right.

(1) $\begin{array}{r} 1.3 \\ \times\,0.4 \end{array}$

(5) $\begin{array}{r} 1.7 \\ \times\,0.6 \end{array}$

(9) $\begin{array}{r} 3.6 \\ \times\,0.4 \end{array}$

(13) $\begin{array}{r} 2.9 \\ \times\,0.8 \end{array}$

(2) $\begin{array}{r} 1.3 \\ \times\,0.6 \end{array}$

(6) $\begin{array}{r} 2.4 \\ \times\,0.3 \end{array}$

(10) $\begin{array}{r} 3.8 \\ \times\,0.5 \end{array}$

(3) $\begin{array}{r} 1.3 \\ \times\,0.8 \end{array}$

(7) $\begin{array}{r} 2.4 \\ \times\,0.9 \end{array}$

(11) $\begin{array}{r} 4.2 \\ \times\,0.7 \end{array}$

(4) $\begin{array}{r} 1.7 \\ \times\,0.4 \end{array}$

(8) $\begin{array}{r} 2.7 \\ \times\,0.3 \end{array}$

(12) $\begin{array}{r} 4.5 \\ \times\,0.4 \end{array}$

2 Multiply.

(1) 1.2
    ×0.7

(2) 5.4
    ×0.3

(3) 2.6
    ×0.9

(4) 3.7
    ×0.4

(5) 4.9
    ×0.5

(6) 7.2
    ×0.8

(7) 5.7
    ×0.3

(8) 4.8
    ×0.6

(9) 12.4
    × 0.7

(10) 13.2
    × 0.6

(11) 23.5
    × 0.4

(12) 24.7
    × 0.5

(13) 32.6
    × 0.8

(14) 45.9
    × 0.2

(15) 38.2
    × 0.4

(16) 54.3
    × 0.9

When you are multiplying two numbers with decimal points, it is very important to put the decimal point in the right place in your answer.

Multiplication of Decimals

Level ★★

Date / /

Name

Score /100

1 Multiply.

5 points per question

Example

① First, calculate 34 × 42.

② Then place the decimal point.

```
    3.4
  × 4.2
    6 8
  1 3 6
1 4.2 8
```

```
    3 4
  × 4 2
    6 8
  1 3 6
1 4 2 8
```

```
    3.4
  × 4.2
1 4.2 8
```

Here, the decimal point is one digit from the right.

Here, the decimal point is also one digit from the right.

Therefore, move this decimal point two digits from the right.

(1)
```
  1.6
× 1.4
```

(2)
```
  1.6
× 1.8
```

(3)
```
  1.6
× 2.4
```

(4)
```
  2.3
× 1.4
```

(5)
```
  2.3
× 2.6
```

(6)
```
  1.8
× 1.7
```

(7)
```
  0.8
× 1.7
```

(8)
```
  0.8
× 2.4
```

(9)
```
  0.9
× 1.5
```

(10)
```
  0.9
× 2.4
```

② Multiply.

5 points per question

(1)　　2.4
　　× 1.8

(4)　　3.7
　　× 2.7

(7)　　4.5
　　× 2.8

(10)　　5.3
　　× 4.5

(2)　　0.6
　　× 1.9

(5)　　0.5
　　× 2.3

(8)　　0.8
　　× 3.6

(3)　　1.9
　　× 4.2

(6)　　3.6
　　× 2.5

(9)　　3.4
　　× 2.6

Good job! Let's move on to the next step.

Multiplication of Decimals

Date / /

Name

Score /100

1 **Multiply.**

5 points per question

Example

① **First, calculate 134 × 26.**

```
  1.3 4
×   2.6
  8 0 4
2 6 8
3.4 8 4
```

```
  1 3 4
×   2 6
  8 0 4
2 6 8
3 4 8 4
```

② **Then place the decimal point.**

```
  1.3 4
×   2.6
3.4 8 4
```

Here, the decimal point is two digits from the right.

Here, the decimal point is one digit from the right.

Therefore, move this decimal point three digits from the right.

(1)
```
  1.3 4
×   2.8
```

(4)
```
  2.3 6
×   1.3
```

(7)
```
  0.8 3
×   1.7
```

(10)
```
  0.4 5
×   3.6
```

(2)
```
  1.2 3
×   2.5
```

(5)
```
  3.5 6
×   2.4
```

(8)
```
  0.6 5
×   3.4
```

(3)
```
  1.6 8
×   1.4
```

(6)
```
  1.8 3
×   1.7
```

(9)
```
  0.7 4
×   2.9
```

2 Multiply.

Example

$$
\begin{array}{r}
2.8 \\
\times\,0.4\,3 \\
\hline
8\,4 \\
1\,1\,2 \\
\hline
1.2\,0\,4
\end{array}
$$

① **First, calculate 28 × 43.**

$$
\begin{array}{r}
2\,8 \\
\times\,4\,3 \\
\hline
8\,4 \\
1\,1\,2 \\
\hline
1\,2\,0\,4
\end{array}
$$

② **Then place the decimal point.**

$$
\begin{array}{r}
2.8 \\
\times\,0.4\,3 \\
\hline
1.2\,0\,4
\end{array}
$$

Here, the decimal point is one digit from the right.

Here, the decimal point is two digits from the right.

Therefore, move this decimal point three digits from the right.

(1)
$$
\begin{array}{r}
2.8 \\
\times\,0.3\,6 \\
\hline
\end{array}
$$

(4)
$$
\begin{array}{r}
3.4 \\
\times\,0.2\,6 \\
\hline
\end{array}
$$

(7)
$$
\begin{array}{r}
3.7 \\
\times\,0.6\,2 \\
\hline
\end{array}
$$

(10)
$$
\begin{array}{r}
3.6 \\
\times\,0.7\,8 \\
\hline
\end{array}
$$

(2)
$$
\begin{array}{r}
1.6 \\
\times\,0.4\,7 \\
\hline
\end{array}
$$

(5)
$$
\begin{array}{r}
4.1 \\
\times\,0.3\,6 \\
\hline
\end{array}
$$

(8)
$$
\begin{array}{r}
5.3 \\
\times\,0.4\,5 \\
\hline
\end{array}
$$

(3)
$$
\begin{array}{r}
2.3 \\
\times\,0.1\,7 \\
\hline
\end{array}
$$

(6)
$$
\begin{array}{r}
2.4 \\
\times\,0.5\,6 \\
\hline
\end{array}
$$

(9)
$$
\begin{array}{r}
4.2 \\
\times\,0.3\,5 \\
\hline
\end{array}
$$

Well done! Let's check to make sure the decimal points are in the right places.

Division of Decimals

16

Date / /

Name

Score

/100

1 **Divide until there is no remainder.**

5 points per question

Example	$120 \div 5 = 24$	$12 \div 5 = 2.4$

(1) $140 \div 4 =$

(2) $14 \div 4 =$

(3) $60 \div 4 =$

(4) $6 \div 4 =$

(5) $160 \div 5 =$

(6) $16 \div 5 =$

(7) $150 \div 6 =$

(8) $15 \div 6 =$

(9) $270 \div 6 =$

(10) $27 \div 6 =$

(11) $200 \div 8 =$

(12) $20 \div 8 =$

2 Divide until there is no remainder.

Example

$$4\overline{)14} \longrightarrow \begin{array}{r} 3.5 \\ 4\overline{)14.0} \\ \underline{12} \\ 20 \\ \underline{20} \\ 0 \end{array}$$

(1)
$$\begin{array}{r} \square.\square \\ 4\overline{)18.0} \end{array}$$

(4)
$$5\overline{)8}$$

(7)
$$\begin{array}{r} \square\square.\square \\ 6\overline{)63} \end{array}$$

(2)
$$4\overline{)6}$$

(5)
$$5\overline{)34}$$

(8)
$$8\overline{)84}$$

(3)
$$5\overline{)12}$$

(6)
$$6\overline{)45}$$

Let's keep dividing until there is no remainder. Hang in there!

Division of Decimals

Date / /

Name

Score /100

1 **Divide until there is no remainder.**

5 points per question

Example

$$5\overline{)24} \longrightarrow 5\overline{)24.0}$$

```
        4.8
  5) 2 4.0
     2 0
       4 0
       4 0
          0
```

$$5\overline{)24.6} \longrightarrow 5\overline{)24.60}$$

```
        4.9 2
  5) 2 4.6 0
     2 0
       4 6
       4 5
         1 0
         1 0
            0
```

(1)
```
5) 1 8
```

(4)
```
4) 2 2.6
```

(7)
```
5) 4 6
```

(2)
```
5) 1 8.7
```

(5)
```
6) 2 7
```

(8)
```
5) 4 6.8
```

(3)
```
4) 2 2
```

(6)
```
6) 2 7.9
```

2 Divide until there is no remainder.

5 points per question

(1)

$4\overline{)14}$

(2)

$4\overline{)14.6}$

(3)

$4\overline{)7.00}$

(4)

$\begin{array}{r} 0.\square\square\square \\ 4\overline{)0.7} \end{array}$

(5)

$4\overline{)9}$

(6)

$4\overline{)0.9}$

(7)

$5\overline{)9}$

(8)

$\begin{array}{r} 0.\square \\ 5\overline{)4} \end{array}$

(9)

$5\overline{)0.4}$

(10)

$8\overline{)14}$

(11)

$8\overline{)6}$

(12)

$8\overline{)0.6}$

Remember to make sure your decimals are in the correct places!

Division of Decimals

Score

/100

Date   /   /

Name

---

1 **Divide until there is no remainder.**

6 points per question

Example

$$
4 \overline{)5.34} \longrightarrow
\begin{array}{r}
1.335 \\
4 \overline{)5.340} \\
\underline{4} \\
13 \\
\underline{12} \\
14 \\
\underline{12} \\
20 \\
\underline{20} \\
0
\end{array}
$$

(1)

$$5 \overline{)8.6}$$

(3)

$$4 \overline{)6.24}$$

(5)

$$6 \overline{)1.59}$$

(2)

$$5 \overline{)8.63}$$

(4)

$$6 \overline{)1.5}$$

(6)

$$4 \overline{)2.98}$$

2 Divide until there is no remainder.

(1)

$4 \overline{) 5.4}$

(2)

$4 \overline{) 0.5\,4}$

(3)

$5 \overline{) 0.7\,2}$

(4)

$6 \overline{) 0.8\,1}$

(5)

$4 \overline{) 0.2\,2}$

(6)

$5 \overline{) 0.4\,6}$

(7)

$8 \overline{) 0.2\,8}$

(8)

$6 \overline{) 0.2\,7}$

If you're not sure about your answer, it never hurts to try again!

Division of Decimals

Date / /

Name

Score /100

1 Divide until there is no remainder.

7 points per question

Example

$$15\overline{)6} \longrightarrow \begin{array}{r} 0.4 \\ 15\overline{)6.0} \\ \underline{6\ 0} \\ 0 \end{array}$$

(1) $15\overline{)9.0}$

(2) $12\overline{)6}$

(3) $14\overline{)7}$

(4) $16\overline{)8}$

(5) $20\overline{)8}$

(6) $15\overline{)12}$

(7) $25\overline{)10}$

(8) $26\overline{)13}$

(9) $35\overline{)21}$

(10) $38\overline{)19}$

2 Divide until there is no remainder.

5 points per question

Example

$$25\overline{)31} \longrightarrow 25\overline{)31.00}$$

$$
\begin{array}{r}
1.24 \\
25{\overline{)31.00}} \\
25 \\
\hline
60 \\
50 \\
\hline
100 \\
100 \\
\hline
0
\end{array}
$$

(1)
$$16\overline{)20}$$

(2)
$$16\overline{)28}$$

(3)
$$16\overline{)12}$$

(4)
$$25\overline{)58}$$

(5)
$$25\overline{)52}$$

(6)
$$25\overline{)12}$$

Great! In order to prevent mistakes, you can check each problem while you are solving it.

Division of Decimals

Date / /

Name

 Score /100

1 **Divide until there is no remainder.**

6 points per question

Example

$$22\overline{)16.5} \longrightarrow 22\overline{)16.50}$$

```
      0.7 5
22) 1 6.5 0
    1 5 4
      1 1 0
      1 1 0
          0
```

(1)

$$15\overline{)12.9}$$

(3)

$$15\overline{)16.2}$$

(5)

$$18\overline{)18.9}$$

(2)

$$15\overline{)21.3}$$

(4)

$$18\overline{)13.5}$$

(6)

$$18\overline{)44.1}$$

2 Divide until there is no remainder.

8 points per question

(1)

$$15\overline{)33.6}$$

(4)

$$35\overline{)36.4}$$

(7)

$$45\overline{)48.6}$$

(2)

$$16\overline{)13.6}$$

(5)

$$24\overline{)34.8}$$

(8)

$$26\overline{)81.9}$$

(3)

$$14\overline{)77.7}$$

(6)

$$32\overline{)75.2}$$

Good job! Let's try something a little different.

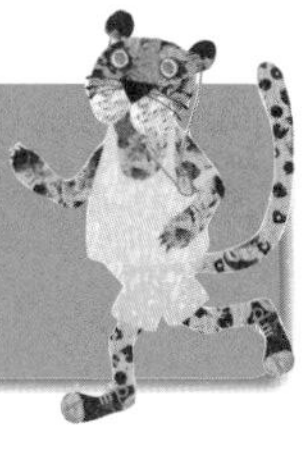

Level ★★

Date   /   /

Name

Score   /100

1 Convert the divisors and dividends into whole numbers as shown in the example below.

4 points per question

Example $30 \overline{)60}$ ⟶ $3 \overline{)6}$ $0.3 \overline{)6}$ ⟶ $3 \overline{)60}$

$1.8 \overline{)3.6}$ ⟶ $18 \overline{)36}$

(1) $40 \overline{)80}$ ⟶ $4 \overline{)}$

(2) $0.4 \overline{)8}$ ⟶ $4 \overline{)}$

(3) $0.4 \overline{)0.8}$ ⟶ $4 \overline{)}$

(4) $0.5 \overline{)4}$ ⟶ $5 \overline{)}$

(5) $0.5 \overline{)0.4}$ ⟶ $5 \overline{)}$

(6) $0.7 \overline{)35}$ ⟶ $7 \overline{)}$

(7) $0.7 \overline{)3.5}$ ⟶ $7 \overline{)}$

(8) $0.8 \overline{)3.2}$ ⟶ $8 \overline{)}$

(9) $1.2 \overline{)72}$ ⟶ $12 \overline{)}$

(10) $1.2 \overline{)7.2}$ ⟶ $12 \overline{)}$

(11) $1.6 \overline{)24}$ ⟶ $16 \overline{)}$

(12) $1.6 \overline{)2.4}$ ⟶ $16 \overline{)}$

(13) $2.1 \overline{)16.8}$ ⟶ $21 \overline{)}$

(14) $2.5 \overline{)13.5}$ ⟶ $25 \overline{)}$

(15) $3.2 \overline{)14.4}$ ⟶ $32 \overline{)}$

(16) $3.6 \overline{)16.2}$ ⟶ $36 \overline{)}$

2 Convert the divisors and dividends into whole numbers as shown in the example below.

2 points per question

Example $0.3 \overline{) 0.15}$ ⟶ $3 \overline{) 1.5}$ $0.03 \overline{) 0.15}$ ⟶ $3 \overline{) 15}$

$1.8 \overline{) 1.26}$ ⟶ $18 \overline{) 12.6}$

(1) $0.4 \overline{) 1.2}$ ⟶ $4 \overline{)}$

(2) $0.4 \overline{) 0.12}$ ⟶ $4 \overline{)}$

(3) $0.7 \overline{) 3.5}$ ⟶ $7 \overline{)}$

(4) $0.7 \overline{) 0.35}$ ⟶ $7 \overline{)}$

(5) $0.8 \overline{) 4.8}$ ⟶ $8 \overline{)}$

(6) $0.8 \overline{) 0.48}$ ⟶ $8 \overline{)}$

(7) $1.4 \overline{) 5.6}$ ⟶ $14 \overline{)}$

(8) $1.4 \overline{) 0.56}$ ⟶ $14 \overline{)}$

(9) $2.1 \overline{) 0.84}$ ⟶ $21 \overline{)}$

(10) $1.8 \overline{) 14.4}$ ⟶ $18 \overline{)}$

(11) $1.8 \overline{) 1.44}$ ⟶ $18 \overline{)}$

(12) $2.3 \overline{) 3.68}$ ⟶ $23 \overline{)}$

(13) $3.5 \overline{) 5.95}$ ⟶ $35 \overline{)}$

(14) $0.16 \overline{) 2.4}$ ⟶ $16 \overline{)}$

(15) $0.16 \overline{) 0.24}$ ⟶ $16 \overline{)}$

(16) $0.24 \overline{) 14.4}$ ⟶ $24 \overline{)}$

(17) $0.24 \overline{) 1.44}$ ⟶ $24 \overline{)}$

(18) $0.32 \overline{) 1.44}$ ⟶ $32 \overline{)}$

Remember to multiply the dividend and the divisor by the same number each time!

1 Divide until there is no remainder.

5 points per question

Example

$$0.6\overline{)2\,4} \longrightarrow 0.6\overline{)2\,4\,0}$$
$$\begin{array}{r} 4\,0 \\ \hline 2\,4 \\ \hline 0 \end{array}$$

$$0.6\overline{)2.4} \longrightarrow 0.6\overline{)2.4}$$
$$\begin{array}{r} 4 \\ \hline 2\,4 \\ \hline 0 \end{array}$$

$$0.6\overline{)0.2\,4} \longrightarrow 0.6\overline{)0.2.4}$$
$$\begin{array}{r} 0.4 \\ \hline 2\,4 \\ \hline 0 \end{array}$$

(1) $0.3\overline{)6}$

(2) $0.3\overline{)0.6}$

(3) $0.3\overline{)0.06}$

(4) $0.4\overline{)2\,4}$

(5) $0.4\overline{)2.4}$

(6) $0.4\overline{)0.24}$

(7) $0.6\overline{)15}$

(8) $0.6\overline{)1.5}$

(9) $0.6\overline{)0.15}$

(10) $0.8\overline{)0.28}$

2 Divide until there is no remainder.

5 points per question

(1)

$0.4\overline{)18}$

(4)

$0.5\overline{)24}$

(7)

$0.6\overline{)45}$

(10)

$0.8\overline{)0.36}$

(2)

$0.4\overline{)1.8}$

(5)

$0.5\overline{)2.4}$

(8)

$0.6\overline{)4.5}$

(3)

$0.4\overline{)0.18}$

(6)

$0.5\overline{)0.24}$

(9)

$0.6\overline{)0.45}$

You're doing great! Did you solve your problems without mistakes?

Level ★★

Score

/ 100

Date / /

Name

1 **Divide until there is no remainder.**

5 points per question

(1)
$$0.4\overline{)132}$$

(2)
$$0.4\overline{)13.2}$$

(3)
$$0.4\overline{)1.32}$$

(4)
$$0.4\overline{)1.84}$$

(5)
$$0.5\overline{)175}$$

(6)
$$0.5\overline{)17.5}$$

(7)
$$0.5\overline{)1.75}$$

(8)
$$0.5\overline{)3.25}$$

(9)
$$0.6\overline{)276}$$

(10)
$$0.6\overline{)27.6}$$

(11)
$$0.6\overline{)2.76}$$

(12)
$$0.6\overline{)3.24}$$

2 Divide.

(1)

$0.3 \overline{)7.5}$

(2)

$0.6 \overline{)2.7}$

(3)

$0.4 \overline{)2.8}$

(4)

$0.5 \overline{)13.5}$

(5)

$0.7 \overline{)25.2}$

(6)

$0.4 \overline{)37.6}$

(7)

$0.5 \overline{)0.4}$

(8)

$0.8 \overline{)2.8}$

(9)

$0.3 \overline{)4.5}$

(10)

$0.8 \overline{)44.8}$

If a problem looks tricky, just think about it a bit more.

Level

Date
/ /

Name

Score
/100

1 Divide until there is no remainder.

5 points per question

Example

$$1.6\overline{)8} \longrightarrow 1.6\overline{)8\,0} \quad \begin{array}{r} 5 \\ \underline{8\,0} \\ 0 \end{array}$$

$$1.6\overline{)0.8} \longrightarrow 1.6\overline{)0.8.0} \quad \begin{array}{r} 0.5 \\ \underline{8\,0} \\ 0 \end{array}$$

(1) $1.5\overline{)6}$

(2) $1.5\overline{)0.6}$

(3) $1.8\overline{)9}$

(4) $1.8\overline{)0.9}$

(5) $1.2\overline{)6}$

(6) $1.2\overline{)0.6}$

(7) $2.5\overline{)5}$

(8) $2.5\overline{)0.5}$

(9) $1.6\overline{)4}$

(10) $1.6\overline{)0.4}$

(11) $2.5\overline{)6}$

(12) $2.5\overline{)0.6}$

2 Divide.

5 points per question

Example

$$1.6\overline{)96} \longrightarrow 1{,}6\overline{)9\,6\,0}$$
$$\phantom{1{,}6)}\underline{9\,6}$$
$$\phantom{1{,}6)9\,}0$$

with quotient 60

$$1.6\overline{)9.6} \longrightarrow 1{,}6\overline{)9{,}6}$$
$$\phantom{1{,}6)}\underline{9\,6}$$
$$\phantom{1{,}6)9}0$$

with quotient 6

$$1.6\overline{)0.96} \longrightarrow 1{,}6\overline{)0{,}9{,}6}$$
$$\phantom{1{,}6)0{,}}\underline{9\,6}$$
$$\phantom{1{,}6)0{,}9}0$$

with quotient 0.6

(1)
$$1.2\overline{)36}$$

(2)
$$1.2\overline{)3.6}$$

(3)
$$1.2\overline{)0.36}$$

(4)
$$1.2\overline{)0.48}$$

(5)
$$1.4\overline{)84}$$

(6)
$$1.4\overline{)8.4}$$

(7)
$$1.4\overline{)0.84}$$

(8)
$$1.4\overline{)0.56}$$

Remember, practice makes perfect!

Division of Decimals

Date   /   /

Name

Score

/100

1 **Divide until there is no remainder.**

5 points per question

(1)
$$1.4\overline{)2\,1}$$

(2)
$$1.4\overline{)2.1}$$

(3)
$$1.4\overline{)0.2\,1}$$

(4)
$$1.8\overline{)0.4\,5}$$

(5)
$$1.5\overline{)3\,6}$$

(6)
$$1.5\overline{)3.6}$$

(7)
$$1.5\overline{)0.3\,6}$$

(8)
$$3.5\overline{)0.5\,6}$$

(9)
$$2.4\overline{)7\,8}$$

(10)
$$2.4\overline{)7.8}$$

(11)
$$2.4\overline{)0.7\,8}$$

(12)
$$1.6\overline{)0.8\,4}$$

2 Divide.

Example

$$1.6\overline{)128} \rightarrow 1.6\overline{)1280} \qquad \begin{array}{r} 80 \\ 128 \\ \hline 0 \end{array}$$

$$1.6\overline{)12.8} \rightarrow 1.6\overline{)12.8} \qquad \begin{array}{r} 8 \\ 128 \\ \hline 0 \end{array}$$

$$1.6\overline{)1.28} \rightarrow 1.6\overline{)1.2.8} \qquad \begin{array}{r} 0.8 \\ 128 \\ \hline 0 \end{array}$$

(1) $1.8\overline{)144}$

(2) $1.8\overline{)14.4}$

(3) $1.8\overline{)1.44}$

(4) $2.4\overline{)1.44}$

(5) $2.6\overline{)104}$

(6) $2.6\overline{)10.4}$

(7) $2.6\overline{)1.04}$

(8) $2.8\overline{)2.52}$

Great! Now let's check your answers.

26 Division of Decimals

Level ★★

Date　　/　　/

Name

Score

/100

1 **Divide until there is no remainder.**

5 points per question

(1)

1.9)2 4 7

(5)

2.6)7 0 2

(9)

3.8)5 5 1

(2)

1.9)2 4.7

(6)

2.6)7 0.2

(10)

3.8)5 5.1

(3)

1.9)2.4 7

(7)

2.6)7.0 2

(11)

3.8)5.5 1

(4)

2.3)3.2 2

(8)

3.2)7.6 8

(12)

3.5)7.8 4

2 Divide until there is no remainder.

4 points per question

(1)

0.6)2.1

(5)

4.5)162

(9)

1.6)5.6

(2)

0.4)0.26

(6)

0.8)5.2

(10)

2.8)2.24

(3)

1.8)4.5

(7)

0.6)2.7

(4)

2.5)0.15

(8)

3.2)5.12

Don't forget to show your parents how far you've come!

Division of Decimals

Date / /

Name

Score /100

1 **Divide until there is no remainder.**

5 points per question

Example

$$1.4\overline{)5.6} \rightarrow 1.4\overline{)5.6}$$
$$\begin{array}{r} 4 \\ 5\ 6 \\ \hline 0 \end{array}$$

$$0.14\overline{)5.6} \rightarrow 0.14\overline{)5.60}$$
$$\begin{array}{r} 4\ 0 \\ 5\ 6 \\ \hline 0 \end{array}$$

$$0.14\overline{)0.56} \rightarrow 0.14\overline{)0.56}$$
$$\begin{array}{r} 4 \\ 5\ 6 \\ \hline 0 \end{array}$$

(1) $1.2\overline{)4.8}$

(2) $0.12\overline{)4.8}$

(3) $0.12\overline{)0.48}$

(4) $0.13\overline{)0.52}$

(5) $1.5\overline{)7.5}$

(6) $0.15\overline{)7.5}$

(7) $0.15\overline{)0.75}$

(8) $0.16\overline{)0.96}$

(9) $1.8\overline{)7.2}$

(10) $0.18\overline{)7.2}$

(11) $0.18\overline{)0.72}$

(12) $0.24\overline{)0.96}$

2 **Divide until there is no remainder.**

4 points per question

(1)
$$1.6\overline{)5.6}$$

(5)
$$1.8\overline{)13.5}$$

(9)
$$1.4\overline{)11.9}$$

(2)
$$1.6\overline{)0.56}$$

(6)
$$1.8\overline{)1.35}$$

(10)
$$2.6\overline{)6.11}$$

(3)
$$0.16\overline{)0.56}$$

(7)
$$0.18\overline{)1.35}$$

(4)
$$0.25\overline{)0.85}$$

(8)
$$2.4\overline{)5.88}$$

Are you getting the hang of decimals?

28
Three Decimals ◆Mixed Calculations

Date   /   /

Name

Level
★★★

Score
/100

1 **Calculate.**

5 points per question

(1) $7 \times 0.4 \times 0.8 =$

(4) $6 \times 1.4 \div 1.2 =$

(2) $1.6 \times 4 \times 0.2 =$

(5) $4.5 \div 5 \times 0.8 =$

(3) $1.8 \times 0.5 \times 1.4 =$

(6) $2.4 \div 0.3 \div 4 =$

2 **Calculate.**

5 points per question

(1) $(2.5 + 1.6) \times 3 =$

(3) $2.8 \times (7.3 - 2.7) =$

(2) $4.2 \div (2.7 + 4.3) =$

(4) $(12.6 - 4.2) \div 3.5 =$

Calculate the expression in the parentheses first.

3 **Calculate.**

5 points per question

(1) $1.7 \times 4 + 0.6 =$

(3) $4.2 \div 1.2 - 0.9 =$

(2) $6.3 - 1.8 \times 2.5 =$

(4) $2.7 + 5.1 \div 3.4 =$

4 **Calculate.**

5 points per question

(1) $2.9 \times 4 - 3.8 =$

(4) $10.3 - 4.5 \div 0.6 =$

(2) $8.4 \div 7 + 0.9 =$

(5) $(4.3 + 2.7) \times 5 =$

(3) $1.6 + 1.6 \times 1.5 =$

(6) $5.4 \div (9.7 - 3.7) =$

Don't forget to check your answers when you're done.

1 **Multiply.**

4 points per question

(1) 3.7
   × 8

(5) 3 0.5
   ×   9

(9) 3 4.9
   × 0.5

(13) 6.9
   × 3.4

(2) 1.9
   × 2 4

(6) 2 8
   × 0.3

(10) 5.2
   × 2.6

(3) 4 3.6
   ×   5

(7) 2 9 3
   × 0.7

(11) 7.4
   × 5 2

(4) 5.8
   × 3 6

(8) 1.5
   × 0.6

(12) 3 7.9
   × 0.4

2 Divide until there is no remainder.

4 points per question

(1) $4\overline{)34}$

(2) $5\overline{)21.6}$

(3) $8\overline{)18}$

(4) $35\overline{)28.7}$

(5) $46\overline{)48.3}$

(6) $0.6\overline{)0.3}$

(7) $0.9\overline{)21.6}$

(8) $1.4\overline{)4.9}$

(9) $2.8\overline{)7}$

(10) $3.5\overline{)56.7}$

(11) $15\overline{)12.3}$

(12) $0.7\overline{)18.2}$

Well done. Are you ready for something a little bit different?

Fractions Review

1 Rewrite the improper fractions as whole numbers.

2 points per question

(1) $\frac{2}{2} =$

(5) $\frac{7}{7} =$

(2) $\frac{3}{3} =$

(6) $\frac{6}{3} =$

(3) $\frac{8}{4} =$

(7) $\frac{9}{9} =$

(4) $\frac{10}{5} =$

(8) $\frac{12}{6} =$

2 Rewrite the improper fractions as mixed numbers.

3 points per question

(1) $\frac{3}{2} =$

(6) $\frac{9}{7} =$

(2) $\frac{4}{3} =$

(7) $\frac{8}{3} =$

(3) $\frac{7}{4} =$

(8) $\frac{11}{9} =$

(4) $\frac{8}{5} =$

(9) $\frac{5}{2} =$

(5) $\frac{7}{6} =$

(10) $\frac{12}{5} =$

3 **Rewrite the improper fractions as mixed numbers or whole numbers.** 3 points per question

(1) $\dfrac{8}{5} =$

(2) $\dfrac{8}{7} =$

(3) $\dfrac{4}{4} =$

(4) $\dfrac{10}{9} =$

(5) $\dfrac{13}{11} =$

(6) $\dfrac{4}{2} =$

(7) $\dfrac{7}{3} =$

(8) $\dfrac{9}{8} =$

(9) $\dfrac{6}{6} =$

(10) $\dfrac{5}{4} =$

(11) $\dfrac{5}{5} =$

(12) $\dfrac{13}{9} =$

(13) $\dfrac{5}{3} =$

(14) $\dfrac{13}{7} =$

(15) $\dfrac{15}{8} =$

(16) $\dfrac{11}{11} =$

(17) $\dfrac{14}{9} =$

(18) $\dfrac{12}{7} =$

OK! Let's review fractions a bit more!

1 Rewrite the improper fractions as mixed numbers or whole numbers. 2 points per question

(1) $\dfrac{7}{5} =$

(2) $\dfrac{8}{3} =$

(3) $\dfrac{5}{4} =$

(4) $\dfrac{9}{7} =$

(5) $\dfrac{10}{9} =$

(6) $\dfrac{3}{3} =$

(7) $\dfrac{6}{3} =$

(8) $\dfrac{4}{4} =$

(9) $\dfrac{10}{5} =$

(10) $\dfrac{14}{7} =$

2 Rewrite the mixed numbers and whole numbers as improper fractions. 2 points per question

(1) $1\dfrac{2}{5} =$

(2) $2\dfrac{2}{3} =$

(3) $1\dfrac{1}{4} =$

(4) $1\dfrac{2}{7} =$

(5) $1\dfrac{1}{9} =$

(6) $1 = \dfrac{\square}{3}$

(7) $2 = \dfrac{\square}{3}$

(8) $1 = \dfrac{\square}{4}$

(9) $2 = \dfrac{\square}{5}$

(10) $2 = \dfrac{\square}{7}$

3 **Rewrite the mixed numbers as improper fractions.**

3 points per question

(1) $1\dfrac{1}{2} =$

(2) $1\dfrac{1}{4} =$

(3) $2\dfrac{1}{3} =$

(4) $2\dfrac{1}{2} =$

(5) $1\dfrac{3}{4} =$

(6) $1\dfrac{2}{5} =$

(7) $1\dfrac{1}{7} =$

(8) $1\dfrac{2}{9} =$

(9) $2\dfrac{1}{5} =$

(10) $2\dfrac{2}{3} =$

(11) $1\dfrac{3}{4} =$

(12) $2\dfrac{3}{4} =$

(13) $1\dfrac{4}{5} =$

(14) $1\dfrac{4}{9} =$

(15) $1\dfrac{2}{11} =$

(16) $1\dfrac{6}{7} =$

(17) $2\dfrac{1}{5} =$

(18) $2\dfrac{1}{6} =$

(19) $1\dfrac{4}{11} =$

(20) $1\dfrac{5}{7} =$

Excellent! Do you remember your fractions now?

Fractions Review

Date / /

Name

Level

Score

/100

1 Rewrite the improper fractions as mixed numbers or whole numbers.   2 points per question

(1) $\dfrac{5}{3} =$

(2) $\dfrac{9}{7} =$

(3) $\dfrac{8}{5} =$

(4) $\dfrac{8}{4} =$

(5) $\dfrac{13}{9} =$

(6) $\dfrac{9}{8} =$

(7) $\dfrac{6}{3} =$

(8) $\dfrac{4}{2} =$

(9) $\dfrac{15}{11} =$

(10) $\dfrac{7}{6} =$

(11) $\dfrac{8}{8} =$

(12) $\dfrac{7}{3} =$

(13) $\dfrac{5}{2} =$

(14) $\dfrac{16}{9} =$

(15) $\dfrac{13}{7} =$

(16) $\dfrac{12}{6} =$

(17) $\dfrac{5}{4} =$

(18) $\dfrac{11}{5} =$

(19) $\dfrac{11}{7} =$

(20) $\dfrac{17}{11} =$

2 **Rewrite the whole numbers as fractions.**

3 points per question

(1) $1 = \dfrac{\boxed{}}{5}$

(2) $1 = \dfrac{\boxed{}}{6}$

(3) $2 = \dfrac{\boxed{}}{3}$

(4) $2 = \dfrac{\boxed{}}{4}$

(5) $2 = \dfrac{\boxed{}}{9}$

(6) $1 = \dfrac{\boxed{}}{8}$

(7) $1 = \dfrac{\boxed{}}{7}$

(8) $2 = \dfrac{\boxed{}}{7}$

3 **Rewrite the mixed numbers as improper fractions.**

3 points per question

(1) $1\dfrac{3}{4} =$

(2) $2\dfrac{2}{3} =$

(3) $1\dfrac{4}{5} =$

(4) $2\dfrac{1}{6} =$

(5) $1\dfrac{1}{2} =$

(6) $1\dfrac{4}{7} =$

(7) $2\dfrac{1}{3} =$

(8) $1\dfrac{5}{9} =$

(9) $1\dfrac{7}{8} =$

(10) $2\dfrac{1}{4} =$

(11) $1\dfrac{6}{7} =$

(12) $1\dfrac{3}{11} =$

Good job. Now it's time for another step forward!

65

33

Addition of Fractions

Level

Date / /

Name

Score

/100

1 **Add.**

5 points per question

Example $\dfrac{4}{7}+\dfrac{2}{7}=\dfrac{6}{7}$ $\dfrac{4}{7}+\dfrac{3}{7}=\dfrac{7}{7}=1$

(1) $\dfrac{1}{5}+\dfrac{3}{5}=$

(6) $\dfrac{5}{7}+\dfrac{2}{7}=$

(2) $\dfrac{2}{5}+\dfrac{3}{5}=\dfrac{\square}{5}=\square$

(7) $\dfrac{4}{9}+\dfrac{1}{9}=$

(3) $\dfrac{4}{5}+\dfrac{1}{5}=$

(8) $\dfrac{4}{9}+\dfrac{5}{9}=$

(4) $\dfrac{2}{7}+\dfrac{4}{7}=$

(9) $\dfrac{8}{11}+\dfrac{2}{11}=$

(5) $\dfrac{3}{7}+\dfrac{4}{7}=$

(10) $\dfrac{8}{11}+\dfrac{3}{11}=$

2 Add.

5 points per question

Example $\frac{4}{7} + \frac{3}{7} = \frac{7}{7} = 1$ $\frac{4}{7} + \frac{5}{7} = \frac{9}{7} = 1\frac{2}{7}$

(1) $\frac{2}{5} + \frac{1}{5} =$

(2) $\frac{2}{5} + \frac{3}{5} =$

(3) $\frac{2}{5} + \frac{4}{5} = \frac{\square}{5} = \square\frac{\square}{5}$

(4) $\frac{3}{5} + \frac{4}{5} =$

(5) $\frac{4}{5} + \frac{2}{5} =$

(6) $\frac{5}{7} + \frac{2}{7} =$

(7) $\frac{5}{7} + \frac{3}{7} =$

(8) $\frac{4}{7} + \frac{5}{7} =$

(9) $\frac{5}{9} + \frac{4}{9} =$

(10) $\frac{5}{9} + \frac{6}{9} =$

Great! Now let's check your answers.

Date   /   /

Name

Score

/100

1 **Add.**

5 points per question

Example $2+\dfrac{3}{7}=2\dfrac{3}{7}$ $3+2\dfrac{1}{7}=5\dfrac{1}{7}$

(1) $1+\dfrac{3}{5}=$

(2) $2+\dfrac{4}{7}=$

(3) $3+\dfrac{5}{9}=$

(4) $4+1\dfrac{2}{5}=$

(5) $5+2\dfrac{3}{7}=$

(6) $\dfrac{2}{3}+3=$

(7) $\dfrac{2}{5}+6=$

(8) $2\dfrac{1}{8}+4=$

(9) $3\dfrac{7}{9}+2=$

(10) $5\dfrac{1}{4}+3=$

2 Add.

Example $2\frac{2}{7} + 1\frac{3}{7} = 3\frac{5}{7}$

(1) $2\frac{1}{5} + \frac{2}{5} =$

(2) $2\frac{1}{5} + 1\frac{3}{5} =$

(3) $1\frac{4}{7} + \frac{1}{7} =$

(4) $1\frac{2}{7} + 2\frac{3}{7} =$

(5) $2\frac{4}{7} + 3\frac{2}{7} =$

(6) $\frac{2}{9} + 2\frac{3}{9} =$

(7) $1\frac{4}{9} + 3\frac{3}{9} =$

(8) $2\frac{3}{9} + 4\frac{5}{9} =$

(9) $\frac{3}{11} + 3\frac{6}{11} =$

(10) $4\frac{7}{11} + \frac{2}{11} =$

Nice job! Let's keep going!

35 Addition of Fractions

Level ★★

Date   /   /

Name

Score

/100

1 **Add.**

5 points per question

Example $2\dfrac{6}{7} + \dfrac{5}{7} = 2\dfrac{11}{7} = 3\dfrac{4}{7}$

(1) $2\dfrac{2}{3} + \dfrac{2}{3} = 2\dfrac{\square}{3} =$

(6) $\dfrac{4}{5} + 1\dfrac{2}{5} =$

(2) $3\dfrac{4}{5} + \dfrac{3}{5} = 3\dfrac{\square}{5} =$

(7) $\dfrac{6}{7} + 2\dfrac{5}{7} =$

(3) $1\dfrac{4}{7} + \dfrac{5}{7} =$

(8) $\dfrac{6}{7} + 3\dfrac{6}{7} =$

(4) $3\dfrac{2}{9} + \dfrac{8}{9} =$

(9) $\dfrac{4}{9} + 2\dfrac{7}{9} =$

(5) $2\dfrac{5}{11} + \dfrac{9}{11} =$

(10) $\dfrac{8}{11} + 3\dfrac{7}{11} =$

2 **Add.**

5 points per question

Example $1\frac{6}{7} + 2\frac{5}{7} = 3\frac{11}{7} = 4\frac{4}{7}$

(1) $1\frac{2}{3} + 2\frac{2}{3} = 3\frac{\square}{3} =$

(6) $2\frac{4}{5} + 1\frac{3}{5} =$

(2) $1\frac{3}{5} + 2\frac{3}{5} =$

(7) $3\frac{4}{5} + 2\frac{4}{5} =$

(3) $2\frac{3}{7} + 3\frac{6}{7} =$

(8) $1\frac{5}{7} + 3\frac{5}{7} =$

(4) $3\frac{7}{9} + 1\frac{7}{9} =$

(9) $2\frac{3}{7} + 3\frac{5}{7} =$

(5) $4\frac{7}{11} + 2\frac{6}{11} =$

(10) $4\frac{4}{9} + 1\frac{7}{9} =$

Just take it step by step.
You're doing very well!

Addition of Fractions

Level

Date / /

Name

Score

/100

---

1 **Add.**

4 points per question

Example $1\frac{3}{7}+2\frac{4}{7}=3\frac{7}{7}=4$

(1) $2\frac{2}{3}+\frac{1}{3}=2\frac{\square}{3}=\square$

(2) $3\frac{3}{5}+\frac{2}{5}=3\frac{\square}{5}=$

(3) $3\frac{1}{5}+1\frac{4}{5}=$

(4) $\frac{2}{7}+3\frac{5}{7}=$

(5) $2\frac{2}{7}+1\frac{5}{7}=$

(6) $1\frac{4}{7}+2\frac{3}{7}=$

(7) $3\frac{1}{7}+1\frac{6}{7}=$

(8) $\frac{1}{8}+2\frac{7}{8}=$

(9) $1\frac{5}{8}+3\frac{3}{8}=$

(10) $2\frac{1}{8}+\frac{7}{8}=$

2 Add.

5 points per question

(1) $\dfrac{2}{9} + \dfrac{5}{9} =$

(2) $\dfrac{4}{7} + \dfrac{6}{7} =$

(3) $\dfrac{3}{11} + \dfrac{8}{11} =$

(4) $2 + 1\dfrac{2}{3} =$

(5) $2\dfrac{1}{3} + \dfrac{2}{3} =$

(6) $1\dfrac{3}{5} + 2\dfrac{3}{5} =$

(7) $2\dfrac{4}{5} + 3 =$

(8) $\dfrac{5}{11} + \dfrac{7}{11} =$

(9) $\dfrac{7}{8} + \dfrac{1}{8} =$

(10) $1\dfrac{6}{7} + 2\dfrac{4}{7} =$

(11) $1\dfrac{8}{9} + 3\dfrac{2}{9} =$

(12) $2\dfrac{7}{11} + 3\dfrac{4}{11} =$

Well done. Have you mastered adding your mixed numbers?

Subtraction of Fractions

Score

Date   /   /

Name

/100

1 Subtract.

4 points per question

Example $\dfrac{4}{5} - \dfrac{1}{5} = \dfrac{3}{5}$ $\dfrac{6}{5} - \dfrac{2}{5} = \dfrac{4}{5}$

(1) $\dfrac{4}{5} - \dfrac{2}{5} =$

(6) $\dfrac{6}{5} - \dfrac{3}{5} =$

(2) $\dfrac{6}{7} - \dfrac{3}{7} =$

(7) $\dfrac{8}{7} - \dfrac{4}{7} =$

(3) $\dfrac{5}{7} - \dfrac{2}{7} =$

(8) $\dfrac{9}{7} - \dfrac{4}{7} =$

(4) $\dfrac{5}{7} - \dfrac{5}{7} =$

(9) $\dfrac{10}{9} - \dfrac{5}{9} =$

(5) $\dfrac{7}{9} - \dfrac{2}{9} =$

(10) $\dfrac{11}{9} - \dfrac{7}{9} =$

2. Write the appropriate number in each box.

5 points per question

(1) $\dfrac{2}{3} + \dfrac{1}{3} = \boxed{}$

(2) $\dfrac{2}{3} + \dfrac{\boxed{}}{3} = 1$

(3) $\dfrac{3}{4} + \dfrac{\boxed{}}{4} = 1$

(4) $\dfrac{2}{5} + \dfrac{\boxed{}}{5} = 1$

(5) $\dfrac{2}{7} + \dfrac{\boxed{}}{7} = 1$

(6) $\dfrac{7}{9} + \dfrac{\boxed{}}{9} = 1$

3. Subtract.

5 points per question

(1) $1 - \dfrac{3}{4} =$

(2) $1 - \dfrac{2}{3} =$

(3) $1 - \dfrac{1}{6} =$

(4) $1 - \dfrac{7}{9} =$

(5) $1 - \dfrac{2}{7} =$

(6) $1 - \dfrac{2}{5} =$

If you make the whole numbers into fractions first, the problem will be much easier to answer!

38 Subtraction of Fractions

Level

Date   /   /

Name

Score

/100

1 **Subtract.**

5 points per question

Example $2\dfrac{3}{5} - \dfrac{1}{5} = 2\dfrac{2}{5}$ $3\dfrac{5}{7} - 2 = 1\dfrac{5}{7}$

(1) $2\dfrac{4}{5} - \dfrac{1}{5} = 2\dfrac{\Box}{5}$

(2) $3\dfrac{3}{5} - \dfrac{2}{5} =$

(3) $2\dfrac{3}{5} - 2 = \dfrac{\Box}{\Box}$

(4) $2\dfrac{3}{5} - \dfrac{3}{5} =$

(5) $3\dfrac{5}{7} - \dfrac{2}{7} =$

(6) $2\dfrac{6}{7} - 2 =$

(7) $3\dfrac{4}{7} - \dfrac{4}{7} =$

(8) $3\dfrac{7}{9} - \dfrac{5}{9} =$

(9) $2\dfrac{8}{9} - \dfrac{3}{9} =$

(10) $3\dfrac{5}{11} - 3 =$

2 **Subtract.**

Example $2\frac{4}{5} - 1\frac{1}{5} = 1\frac{3}{5}$

(1) $2\frac{3}{5} - 1\frac{1}{5} = 1\frac{\square}{5}$

(6) $2\frac{5}{7} - 1\frac{5}{7} =$

(2) $2\frac{4}{5} - 1\frac{3}{5} =$

(7) $3\frac{5}{9} - 1\frac{1}{9} =$

(3) $2\frac{3}{5} - 2\frac{1}{5} =$

(8) $4\frac{8}{9} - 2\frac{3}{9} =$

(4) $3\frac{4}{7} - 1\frac{3}{7} =$

(9) $5\frac{4}{9} - 4\frac{3}{9} =$

(5) $3\frac{5}{7} - 1\frac{3}{7} =$

(10) $4\frac{8}{11} - 1\frac{5}{11} =$

Excellent! Don't forget to check your answers.

Subtraction of Fractions

Level

Score

/100

1 Subtract.

5 points per question

Example $2 - \dfrac{3}{5} = 1\dfrac{2}{5}$

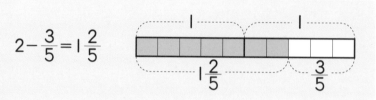

$1\dfrac{2}{5}$ $\dfrac{3}{5}$

(1) $2 - \dfrac{2}{5} = 1\dfrac{\square}{5}$

(2) $2 - \dfrac{4}{5} =$

(3) $3 - \dfrac{2}{7} =$

(4) $3 - \dfrac{4}{7} =$

(5) $3 - \dfrac{4}{5} =$

(6) $4 - \dfrac{3}{7} =$

(7) $4 - \dfrac{3}{4} =$

(8) $4 - \dfrac{1}{5} =$

(9) $2 - \dfrac{2}{9} =$

(10) $4 - \dfrac{2}{9} =$

2 Subtract.

Example $3 - 1\frac{1}{4} = 1\frac{3}{4}$

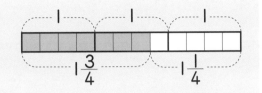

(1) $3 - 1\frac{2}{5} = 1\frac{\square}{5}$

(2) $4 - 1\frac{2}{5} =$

(3) $5 - 1\frac{4}{5} =$

(4) $6 - 1\frac{1}{5} =$

(5) $5 - 2\frac{3}{5} =$

(6) $3 - 1\frac{3}{7} =$

(7) $4 - 1\frac{5}{7} =$

(8) $4 - 2\frac{6}{7} =$

(9) $4 - 2\frac{5}{9} =$

(10) $6 - 3\frac{2}{9} =$

Great job! Let's keep going!

Subtraction of Fractions

Level

Date / /

Name

Score /100

1 Write the appropriate number in each box as shown in the example below.

5 points per question

Example $2\frac{2}{3}=1\frac{5}{3}$ $3\frac{3}{5}=2\frac{8}{5}$

(1) $2\frac{4}{7}=1\frac{\boxed{}}{7}$

(2) $2\frac{5}{7}=1\frac{\boxed{}}{7}$

(3) $2\frac{6}{7}=1\frac{\boxed{}}{7}$

(4) $3\frac{4}{7}=2\frac{\boxed{}}{7}$

(5) $3\frac{6}{7}=2\frac{\boxed{}}{7}$

(6) $3\frac{2}{5}=2\frac{\boxed{}}{5}$

(7) $4\frac{4}{5}=3\frac{\boxed{}}{5}$

(8) $5\frac{3}{5}=4\frac{\boxed{}}{5}$

(9) $5\frac{4}{5}=4\frac{\boxed{}}{5}$

(10) $5\frac{1}{6}=4\frac{\boxed{}}{6}$

2 Subtract.

Example

$$3\frac{2}{5} - \frac{4}{5} = 2\frac{7}{5} - \frac{4}{5}$$

$$= 2\frac{3}{5}$$

(1) $3\frac{1}{5} - \frac{4}{5} = 2\frac{6}{5} - \frac{4}{5}$

$$= 2\frac{\boxed{}}{5}$$

(2) $3\frac{2}{7} - \frac{5}{7} = 2\frac{\boxed{}}{7} - \frac{5}{7}$

$$=$$

(3) $3\frac{3}{7} - \frac{5}{7} = 2\frac{\boxed{}}{7} - \frac{5}{7}$

$$=$$

(4) $3\frac{4}{7} - \frac{5}{7} =$

(5) $3\frac{3}{7} - \frac{6}{7} =$

(6) $4\frac{1}{5} - \frac{3}{5} =$

(7) $4\frac{2}{5} - \frac{3}{5} =$

(8) $4\frac{1}{5} - \frac{2}{5} =$

(9) $5\frac{1}{5} - \frac{4}{5} =$

(10) $5\frac{2}{5} - \frac{4}{5} =$

If you end up with an improper fraction, convert it to a mixed number for the final answer.

81

1 **Subtract.**

4 points per question

(1) $3\dfrac{2}{7} - 1\dfrac{5}{7} = 2\dfrac{\square}{7} - 1\dfrac{5}{7}$

$\quad\quad = $

(2) $4\dfrac{1}{5} - 1\dfrac{2}{5} = $

(3) $3\dfrac{1}{7} - 1\dfrac{3}{7} = $

(4) $4\dfrac{3}{7} - 1\dfrac{4}{7} = $

(5) $4\dfrac{2}{7} - 2\dfrac{4}{7} = $

(6) $5\dfrac{2}{7} - 2\dfrac{6}{7} = $

(7) $6\dfrac{1}{5} - 1\dfrac{3}{5} = $

(8) $5\dfrac{3}{8} - 3\dfrac{6}{8} = $

(9) $3\dfrac{2}{7} - 1\dfrac{3}{7} = $

(10) $6\dfrac{2}{9} - 3\dfrac{4}{9} = $

2 **Subtract.**

(1) $\dfrac{3}{5} - \dfrac{1}{5} =$

(2) $1 - \dfrac{3}{7} =$

(3) $\dfrac{10}{9} - \dfrac{2}{9} =$

(4) $3\dfrac{5}{7} - 1\dfrac{2}{7} =$

(5) $3\dfrac{2}{3} - \dfrac{1}{3} =$

(6) $4\dfrac{8}{9} - 4 =$

(7) $1 - \dfrac{1}{8} =$

(8) $\dfrac{13}{11} - \dfrac{7}{11} =$

(9) $3\dfrac{2}{7} - \dfrac{5}{7} =$

(10) $4\dfrac{3}{7} - 1\dfrac{6}{7} =$

(11) $3 - 1\dfrac{3}{5} =$

(12) $5\dfrac{1}{9} - 2\dfrac{5}{9} =$

Have you mastered your subtraction with mixed numbers?

Three Fractions ◆Mixed Calculations

Date / /

Name

Level

Score
/100

1 **Calculate.**

5 points per question

(1) $\dfrac{2}{7} + \dfrac{1}{7} + \dfrac{3}{7} =$

(5) $\dfrac{2}{7} + \dfrac{6}{7} - \dfrac{3}{7} =$

(2) $\dfrac{3}{7} + \dfrac{2}{7} + \dfrac{5}{7} =$

(6) $\dfrac{5}{9} + \dfrac{3}{9} - \dfrac{4}{9} =$

(3) $\dfrac{2}{9} + \dfrac{4}{9} + \dfrac{1}{9} =$

(7) $\dfrac{4}{5} - \dfrac{2}{5} + \dfrac{1}{5} =$

(4) $\dfrac{2}{9} + \dfrac{5}{9} + \dfrac{4}{9} =$

(8) $\dfrac{8}{11} - \dfrac{5}{11} + \dfrac{7}{11} =$

2 Calculate.

6 points per question

(1) $\dfrac{6}{7} - \dfrac{3}{7} - \dfrac{1}{7} =$

(6) $\dfrac{7}{11} - \dfrac{4}{11} + \dfrac{8}{11} =$

(2) $\dfrac{10}{9} - \dfrac{4}{9} - \dfrac{2}{9} =$

(7) $\dfrac{3}{7} + \dfrac{5}{7} - \dfrac{4}{7} =$

(3) $\dfrac{14}{11} - \dfrac{5}{11} - \dfrac{4}{11} =$

(8) $\dfrac{3}{7} + \left(\dfrac{5}{7} - \dfrac{4}{7} \right) = \dfrac{3}{7} + \dfrac{\square}{7} =$

(4) $\dfrac{4}{5} + \dfrac{3}{5} - \dfrac{2}{5} =$

(9) $\dfrac{6}{7} - \left(\dfrac{2}{7} + \dfrac{3}{7} \right) =$

(5) $\dfrac{8}{9} - \dfrac{5}{9} + \dfrac{7}{9} =$

(10) $\dfrac{6}{7} - \dfrac{2}{7} - \dfrac{3}{7} =$

Are you ready to review what you've learned?

Fractions Review

Date   /   /

Name

Score
/100

1 **Add.**

4 points per question

(1) $\dfrac{4}{7} + \dfrac{2}{7} =$

(2) $\dfrac{3}{5} + \dfrac{2}{5} =$

(3) $\dfrac{2}{9} + \dfrac{8}{9} =$

(4) $1 + \dfrac{5}{6} =$

(5) $2\dfrac{4}{9} + 3 =$

(6) $1\dfrac{3}{7} + \dfrac{1}{7} =$

(7) $\dfrac{7}{8} + \dfrac{1}{8} =$

(8) $\dfrac{6}{11} + \dfrac{7}{11} =$

(9) $\dfrac{2}{9} + 2\dfrac{3}{9} =$

(10) $3\dfrac{2}{9} + \dfrac{8}{9} =$

(11) $1\dfrac{5}{7} + 2\dfrac{4}{7} =$

(12) $1\dfrac{3}{8} + 3\dfrac{5}{8} =$

2 **Subtract.**

(1) $\dfrac{5}{9} - \dfrac{4}{9} =$

(2) $\dfrac{7}{5} - \dfrac{3}{5} =$

(3) $1 - \dfrac{2}{3} =$

(4) $2\dfrac{3}{5} - \dfrac{1}{5} =$

(5) $3\dfrac{5}{7} - 2 =$

(6) $2\dfrac{7}{9} - \dfrac{5}{9} =$

(7) $2\dfrac{6}{7} - 1\dfrac{3}{7} =$

(8) $1 - \dfrac{5}{6} =$

(9) $2 - \dfrac{4}{7} =$

(10) $\dfrac{12}{11} - \dfrac{8}{11} =$

(11) $4 - 1\dfrac{3}{5} =$

(12) $2\dfrac{2}{7} - \dfrac{4}{7} =$

(13) $3\dfrac{2}{9} - 1\dfrac{4}{9} =$

Congratulations! You are ready for **Grade 6 Fractions**!

Answer Key — Grade 5 Decimals & Fractions

1 Multiplication Review
pp 2, 3

1
- (1) 188
- (2) 249
- (3) 288
- (4) 305
- (5) 342
- (6) 280
- (7) 246
- (8) 560
- (9) 2730
- (10) 5292
- (11) 3663
- (12) 5024

2
- (1) 432
- (2) 925
- (3) 1064
- (4) 1664
- (5) 3834
- (6) 1280
- (7) 1680
- (8) 1794
- (9) 4070
- (10) 8265
- (11) 2924
- (12) 4307
- (13) 4067

2 Division Review
pp 4, 5

1
- (1) 21 R 1
- (2) 17 R 2
- (3) 14 R 2
- (4) 14
- (5) 12 R 6
- (6) 12 R 3
- (7) 89
- (8) 86 R 2
- (9) 123 R 3
- (10) 131
- (11) 141 R 3
- (12) 97 R 8

2
- (1) 4
- (2) 3 R 4
- (3) 6
- (4) 9
- (5) 15 R 22
- (6) 8 R 38
- (7) 7 R 3
- (8) 14 R 18
- (9) 16 R 13
- (10) 9 R 14

3 Decimals Review ◆ Addition & Subtraction
pp 6, 7

1
- (1) 1.2
- (2) 4.5
- (3) 8.1
- (4) 9
- (5) 10.4
- (6) 22.3
- (7) 13.46
- (8) 2.68
- (9) 4.32
- (10) 18.34
- (11) 5.08
- (12) 14.3

2
- (1) 1.8
- (2) 2
- (3) 1.5
- (4) 6.2
- (5) 9.3
- (6) 10.6
- (7) 2.57
- (8) 0.34
- (9) 2.46
- (10) 2.14
- (11) 2.25
- (12) 2.8
- (13) 0.48

4 Mixed Review
pp 8, 9

1
- (1) 564
- (2) 144
- (3) 2100
- (4) 4466

2
- (1) 1550
- (2) 4176
- (3) 3220
- (4) 2622

3
- (1) 14 R 2
- (2) 97 R 6
- (3) 237 R 2
- (4) 134 R 2

4
- (1) 5 R 10
- (2) 4 R 3
- (3) 8 R 68
- (4) 37 R 12
- (5) 9
- (6) 7 R 9

5
- (1) 3.2
- (2) 21.7
- (3) 9.12
- (4) 3.6
- (5) 0.8
- (6) 1.78

Advice
If you scored over 85 on this section, review your mistakes and move on to the next section.

If you scored between 75 and 84 on this section, review the beginning of this book before moving on.

If you scored less than 74 on this section, it might be a good idea to go back to our "G4 Multiplication," "Grade 4 Division," and "Grade 4 Decimals & Fractions" books and do an extended review before continuing.

5 Decimals ◆ ×10&100, ÷10&100
pp 10, 11

1
- (1) 3.5
- (2) 4.8
- (3) 3.45
- (4) 6.27
- (5) 0.24
- (6) 42.3
- (7) 423
- (8) 27
- (9) 27.5
- (10) 3.8
- (11) 2.95
- (12) 5.6
- (13) 32
- (14) 41.6
- (15) 84
- (16) 270
- (17) 0.76
- (18) 4.5
- (19) 276
- (20) 647

2
- (1) 4.3
- (2) 6.5
- (3) 43.5
- (4) 62.8
- (5) 0.38
- (6) 3.85
- (7) 0.385
- (8) 0.46
- (9) 2.75
- (10) 0.054
- (11) 39.4
- (12) 5.3
- (13) 0.32
- (14) 4.26
- (15) 0.418
- (16) 0.064
- (17) 2.73
- (18) 0.159
- (19) 0.086
- (20) 0.0647

Advice
Always remember to think about the placement of the decimal point when multiplying and dividing decimals.

6 Multiplication of Decimals
pp 12, 13

1
- (1) 0.8
- (2) 1.2
- (3) 1.6
- (4) 2.4
- (5) 3.2
- (6) 4
- (7) 1.2
- (8) 1.8
- (9) 2.4
- (10) 4.2
- (11) 1.4
- (12) 2.8
- (13) 0.6
- (14) 1.6
- (15) 3.6
- (16) 4.5
- (17) 2
- (18) 3.5
- (19) 4
- (20) 7.2

2
- (1) 4.8
- (2) 6
- (3) 9.6
- (4) 12
- (5) 4.6
- (6) 6.9
- (7) 13.8
- (8) 2.8
- (9) 4.2
- (10) 8.4
- (11) 6.2
- (12) 12.4
- (13) 7.2
- (14) 12
- (15) 3.2
- (16) 6.4
- (17) 7.2
- (18) 14.4
- (19) 7.5
- (20) 10

7 Multiplication of Decimals
pp 14, 15

1
- (1) 5.2
- (2) 7.8
- (3) 10.4
- (4) 4.8
- (5) 8
- (6) 7.2
- (7) 14.4
- (8) 14.4
- (9) 29.4
- (10) 17.4
- (11) 5.6
- (12) 21.5
- (13) 25.2

2
- (1) 7.2
- (2) 16.2
- (3) 21.6
- (4) 14
- (5) 6.3
- (6) 28.8
- (7) 34.8
- (8) 39.2
- (9) 37.2
- (10) 64
- (11) 42.8
- (12) 98.4
- (13) 245.6
- (14) 255
- (15) 145.6
- (16) 246.6

8 Multiplication of Decimals pp 16, 17

1
(1) 1.28 × 3 = 3.84
(2) 1.28 × 4 = 5.12
(3) 1.28 × 5 = 6.40
(4) 2.14 × 2 = 4.28
(5) 2.14 × 6 = 12.84
(6) 3.26 × 3 = 9.78
(7) 3.26 × 5 = 16.30
(8) 1.63 × 2 = 3.26
(9) 1.24 × 7 = 8.68
(10) 2.76 × 3 = 8.28
(11) 4.23 × 4 = 16.92
(12) 3.82 × 5 = 19.10
(13) 2.74 × 9 = 24.66

2
(1) 3.72
(2) 6.4
(3) 0.75 × 3 = 2.25
(4) 2.07 × 4 = 8.28
(5) 3.84
(6) 1.95
(7) 21.42
(8) 4.32
(9) 9.84
(10) 20.15
(11) 5.52
(12) 3.84 × 5 = 19.20
(13) 16.24
(14) 0.47 × 6 = 2.82
(15) 0.047 × 6 = 0.282
(16) 0.944

9 Multiplication of Decimals pp 18, 19

1
(1) 12 × 0.7 = 8.4
(2) 12 × 0.8 = 9.6
(3) 18 × 0.7 = 12.6
(4) 18 × 0.9 = 16.2
(5) 25 × 0.7 = 17.5
(6) 25 × 0.4 = 10.0
(7) 25 × 0.9 = 22.5
(8) 29 × 0.4 = 11.6
(9) 36 × 0.4 = 14.4
(10) 37 × 0.4 = 14.8
(11) 42 × 0.7 = 29.4
(12) 43 × 0.5 = 21.5
(13) 28 × 0.9 = 25.2

2
(1) 7.2
(2) 16.2
(3) 20.8
(4) 14
(5) 6.3
(6) 28.8
(7) 16.8
(8) 37.6
(9) 37.2
(10) 76.8
(11) 164.5
(12) 98.4
(13) 261.6
(14) 273.6
(15) 148.8
(16) 434.4

10 Multiplication of Decimals pp 20, 21

1
(1) 19.2
(2) 36.8
(3) 32.2
(4) 41.4
(5) 57.5
(6) 54.4
(7) 102.6
(8) 71.4
(9) 115
(10) 145.6

2
(1) 22.4
(2) 30.6
(3) 31.2
(4) 44.2
(5) 43.5
(6) 81.7
(7) 80
(8) 102.6
(9) 162
(10) 151.2

11 Multiplication of Decimals pp 22, 23

1
(1) 1.36 × 14: 544, 136, 19.04
(2) 1.48 × 13: 444, 148, 19.24
(3) 2.13 × 18: 1704, 213, 38.34
(4) 41.28
(5) 45.24
(6) 57.04
(7) 81.9
(8) 82.62
(9) 159.12
(10) 140.84

2
(1) 0.6 × 14: 24, 6, 8.4
(2) 0.8 × 17: 56, 8, 13.6
(3) 0.7 × 14: 28, 7, 9.8
(4) 18.2
(5) 13.5
(6) 9.2
(7) 16.8
(8) 25.6
(9) 30.6
(10) 32.2

12 Multiplication of Decimals pp 24, 25

1
(1) 0.36 × 14: 144, 36, 5.04
(2) 0.28 × 13: 84, 28, 3.64
(3) 0.32 × 16: 192, 32, 5.12
(4) 0.25 × 14: 100, 25, 3.50
(5) 0.43 × 15: 215, 43, 6.45
(6) 0.32 × 27: 224, 64, 8.64
(7) 12.88
(8) 11.28
(9) 12.48
(10) 13.52

2
(1) 0.8 × 0.2 = 0.16
(2) 0.8 × 0.6 = 0.48
(3) 0.6 × 0.4 = 0.24
(4) 0.42
(5) 0.45
(6) 0.72
(7) 0.42
(8) 0.63
(9) 0.32
(10) 0.2
(11) 0.35
(12) 0.4

13 Multiplication of Decimals

pp 26, 27

1

(1)
```
    1.3
  × 0.4
  0.5 2
```
(5)
```
    1.7
  × 0.6
  1.0 2
```
(9)
```
    3.6
  × 0.4
  1.4 4
```
(13)
```
    2.9
  × 0.8
  2.3 2
```

(2)
```
    1.3
  × 0.6
  0.7 8
```
(6)
```
    2.4
  × 0.3
  0.7 2
```
(10)
```
    3.8
  × 0.5
  1.9 0
```

(3)
```
    1.3
  × 0.8
  1.0 4
```
(7)
```
    2.4
  × 0.9
  2.1 6
```
(11)
```
    4.2
  × 0.7
  2.9 4
```

(4)
```
    1.7
  × 0.4
  0.6 8
```
(8)
```
    2.7
  × 0.3
  0.8 1
```
(12)
```
    4.5
  × 0.4
  1.8 0
```

2
(1) 0.84   (5) 2.45   (9) 8.68   (13) 26.08
(2) 1.62   (6) 5.76   (10) 7.92   (14) 9.18
(3) 2.34   (7) 1.71   (11) 9.4   (15) 15.28
(4) 1.48   (8) 2.88   (12) 12.35   (16) 48.87

14 Multiplication of Decimals

pp 28, 29

1

(1)
```
    1.6
  × 1.4
    6 4
  1 6
  2.2 4
```
(4)
```
    2.3
  × 1.4
    9 2
  2 3
  3.2 2
```
(7)
```
    0.8
  × 1.7
    5 6
  8
  1.3 6
```
(10)
```
    0.9
  × 2.4
    3 6
  1 8
  2.1 6
```

(2)
```
    1.6
  × 1.8
  1 2 8
  1 6
  2.8 8
```
(5)
```
    2.3
  × 2.6
  1 3 8
  4 6
  5.9 8
```
(8)
```
    0.8
  × 2.4
    3 2
  1 6
  1.9 2
```

(3)
```
    1.6
  × 2.4
    6 4
  3 2
  3.8 4
```
(6)
```
    1.8
  × 1.7
  1 2 6
  1 8
  3.0 6
```
(9)
```
    0.9
  × 1.5
    4 5
  9
  1.3 5
```

2
(1) 4.32   (4) 9.99   (7) 12.6   (10) 23.85
(2) 1.14   (5) 1.15   (8) 2.88
(3) 7.98   (6) 9   (9) 8.84

15 Multiplication of Decimals

pp 30, 31

1

(1)
```
    1.3 4
  ×   2.8
  1 0 7 2
  2 6 8
  3.7 5 2
```
(4)
```
    2.3 6
  ×   1.3
    7 0 8
  2 3 6
  3.0 6 8
```
(7)
```
    0.8 3
  ×   1.7
    5 8 1
  8 3
  1.4 1 1
```
(10)
```
    0.4 5
  ×   3.6
    2 7 0
  1 3 5
  1.6 2 0
```

(2)
```
    1.2 3
  ×   2.5
    6 1 5
  2 4 6
  3.0 7 5
```
(5)
```
    3.5 6
  ×   2.4
  1 4 2 4
  7 1 2
  8.5 4 4
```
(8)
```
    0.6 5
  ×   3.4
    2 6 0
  1 9 5
  2.2 1 0
```

(3)
```
    1.6 8
  ×   1.4
    6 7 2
  1 6 8
  2.3 5 2
```
(6)
```
    1.8 3
  ×   1.7
  1 2 8 1
  1 8 3
  3.1 1 1
```
(9)
```
    0.7 4
  ×   2.9
    6 6 6
  1 4 8
  2.1 4 6
```

2

(1)
```
    2.8
  × 0.3 6
  1 6 8
  8 4
  1.0 0 8
```
(4)
```
    3.4
  × 0.2 6
  2 0 4
  6 8
  0.8 8 4
```
(7)
```
    3.7
  × 0.6 2
    7 4
  2 2 2
  2.2 9 4
```
(10)
```
    3.6
  × 0.7 8
  2 8 8
  2 5 2
  2.8 0 8
```

(2)
```
    1.6
  × 0.4 7
  1 1 2
  6 4
  0.7 5 2
```
(5)
```
    4.1
  × 0.3 6
  2 4 6
  1 2 3
  1.4 7 6
```
(8)
```
    5.3
  × 0.4 5
  2 6 5
  2 1 2
  2.3 8 5
```

(3)
```
    2.3
  × 0.1 7
  1 6 1
  2 3
  0.3 9 1
```
(6)
```
    2.4
  × 0.5 6
  1 4 4
  1 2 0
  1.3 4 4
```
(9)
```
    4.2
  × 0.3 5
  2 1 0
  1 2 6
  1.4 7 0
```

16 Division of Decimals

pp 32, 33

1
(1) 35   (7) 25
(2) 3.5   (8) 2.5
(3) 15   (9) 45
(4) 1.5   (10) 4.5
(5) 32   (11) 25
(6) 3.2   (12) 2.5

2

(1)
```
       4.5
  4)1 8.0
    1 6
      2 0
      2 0
        0
```
(4)
```
      1.6
  5)8
    5
    3 0
    3 0
      0
```
(7)
```
      1 0.5
  6)6 3
    6
      3 0
      3 0
        0
```

(2)
```
      1.5
  4)6
    4
    2 0
    2 0
      0
```
(5)
```
      6.8
  5)3 4
    3 0
      4 0
      4 0
        0
```
(8)
```
      1 0.5
  8)8 4
    8
      4 0
      4 0
        0
```

(3)
```
      2.4
  5)1 2
    1 0
      2 0
      2 0
        0
```
(6)
```
      7.5
  6)4 5
    4 2
      3 0
      3 0
        0
```

17 Division of Decimals

pp 34, 35

1

(1)
```
       3.6
  5)1 8.0
    1 5
      3 0
      3 0
        0
```
(4)
```
      5.6 5
  4)2 2.6
    2 0
      2 6
      2 4
        2 0
        2 0
          0
```
(7)
```
      9.2
  5)4 6
    4 5
      1 0
      1 0
        0
```

(2)
```
       3.7 4
  5)1 8.7
    1 5
      3 7
      3 5
        2 0
        2 0
          0
```
(5)
```
      4.5
  6)2 7
    2 4
      3 0
      3 0
        0
```
(8)
```
      9.3 6
  5)4 6.8
    4 5
      1 8
      1 5
        3 0
        3 0
          0
```

(3) 5.5   (6) 4.6 5

2
(1) 3.5 (5) 2.25 (9) 0.08
(2) 3.65 (6) 0.225 (10) 1.75
(3) 1.75 (7) 1.8 (11) 0.75
(4) 0.☐75 (8) 0.8 (12) 0.075

18 Division of Decimals
pp 36, 37

1
(1)
```
    1.72
 5)8.6
    5
    36
    35
     10
     10
      0
```
(3)
```
    1.56
 4)6.24
    4
    22
    20
     24
     24
      0
```
(5)
```
    0.265
 6)1.59
    12
    39
    36
     30
     30
      0
```
(2)
```
    1.726
 5)8.63
    5
    36
    35
     13
     10
      30
      30
       0
```
(4)
```
    0.25
 6)1.5
    12
    30
    30
     0
```
(6)
```
    0.745
 4)2.98
    28
    18
    16
     20
     20
      0
```

2
(1)
```
    1.35
 4)5.4
    4
    14
    12
     20
     20
      0
```
(4)
```
    0.135
 6)0.81
    6
    21
    18
     30
     30
      0
```
(7)
```
    0.035
 8)0.28
    24
    40
    40
     0
```
(2)
```
    0.135
 4)0.54
    4
    14
    12
     20
     20
      0
```
(5)
```
    0.055
 4)0.22
    20
    20
    20
     0
```
(8)
```
    0.045
 6)0.27
    24
    30
    30
     0
```
(3)
```
    0.144
 5)0.72
    5
    22
    20
     20
     20
      0
```
(6)
```
    0.092
 5)0.46
    45
    10
    10
     0
```

19 Division of Decimals
pp 38, 39

1
(1)
```
    0.6
 15)9.0
    90
     0
```
(5) 0.4   (9) 0.6
(2) 0.5   (6) 0.8   (10) 0.5
(3) 0.5   (7) 0.4
(4) 0.5   (8) 0.5

2
(1)
```
    1.25
 16)20.00
    16
    40
    32
     80
     80
      0
```
(3)
```
    0.75
 16)12.00
    112
     80
     80
      0
```
(5) 2.08
(2)
```
    1.75
 16)28.00
    16
    120
    112
      80
      80
       0
```
(4)
```
    2.32
 25)58.00
    50
    80
    75
     50
     50
      0
```
(6) 0.48

20 Division of Decimals
pp 40, 41

1
(1)
```
    0.86
 15)12.9
    120
     90
     90
      0
```
(3)
```
    1.08
 15)16.2
    15
    120
    120
      0
```
(5) 1.05
(2)
```
    1.42
 15)21.3
    15
    63
    60
     30
     30
      0
```
(4)
```
    0.75
 18)13.5
    126
     90
     90
      0
```
(6) 2.45

2
(1) 2.24   (4) 1.04   (7) 1.08
(2) 0.85   (5) 1.45   (8) 3.15
(3) 5.55   (6) 2.35

21 Division of Decimals
pp 42, 43

1
(1) 40)80 → 4)8
(2) 0.4)8 → 4)80
(3) 0.4)0.8 → 4)8
(4) 0.5)4 → 5)40
(5) 0.5)0.4 → 5)4
(6) 0.7)35 → 7)350
(7) 0.7)3.5 → 7)35
(8) 0.8)3.2 → 8)32
(9) 1.2)72 → 12)720
(10) 1.2)7.2 → 12)72
(11) 1.6)24 → 16)240
(12) 1.6)2.4 → 16)24
(13) 2.1)16.8 → 21)168
(14) 2.5)13.5 → 25)135
(15) 3.2)14.4 → 32)144
(16) 3.6)16.2 → 36)162

2
(1) 0.4)1.2 → 4)12
(2) 0.4)0.12 → 4)1.2
(3) 0.7)3.5 → 7)35
(4) 0.7)0.35 → 7)3.5
(5) 0.8)4.8 → 8)48
(6) 0.8)0.48 → 8)4.8
(7) 1.4)5.6 → 14)56
(8) 1.4)0.56 → 14)5.6
(9) 2.1)0.84 → 21)8.4
(10) 1.8)14.4 → 18)144
(11) 1.8)1.44 → 18)14.4
(12) 2.3)3.68 → 23)36.8
(13) 3.5)5.95 → 35)59.5
(14) 0.16)2.4 → 16)240
(15) 0.16)0.24 → 16)24
(16) 0.24)14.4 → 24)1440
(17) 0.24)1.44 → 24)144
(18) 0.32)1.44 → 32)144

22 Division of Decimals — pp 44, 45

1

(1)
```
        2 0
0.3)6 0
    6 0
        0
```

(4)
```
          6 0
0.4)2 4 0
    2 4
        0
```

(7)
```
          2 5
0.6)1 5 0
    1 2
      3 0
      3 0
        0
```

(10)
```
        0.3 5
0.8)0.2.8
      2 4
        4 0
        4 0
          0
```

(2)
```
          2
0.3)0.6
    6
    0
```

(5)
```
          6
0.4)2.4
    2 4
      0
```

(8)
```
        2.5
0.6)1.5
    1 2
      3 0
      3 0
        0
```

(3)
```
        0.2
0.3)0.0.6
      6
      0
```

(6)
```
        0.6
0.4)0.2.4
      2 4
        0
```

(9)
```
        0.2 5
0.6)0.1.5
      1 2
        3 0
        3 0
          0
```

2

(1) 45	(4) 48	(7) 75	(10) 0.45
(2) 4.5	(5) 4.8	(8) 7.5	
(3) 0.45	(6) 0.48	(9) 0.75	

23 Division of Decimals — pp 46, 47

1

(1) 330	(5) 350	(9) 460
(2) 33	(6) 35	(10) 46
(3) 3.3	(7) 3.5	(11) 4.6
(4) 4.6	(8) 6.5	(12) 5.4

2

(1) 25	(5) 36	(9) 15
(2) 4.5	(6) 94	(10) 56
(3) 7	(7) 0.8	
(4) 27	(8) 3.5	

24 Division of Decimals — pp 48, 49

1

(1)
```
          4
1.5)6 0
    6 0
      0
```

(5)
```
          5
1.2)6 0
    6 0
      0
```

(9) 2.5

(2)
```
        0.4
1.5)0.6.0
    6 0
      0
```

(6)
```
        0.5
1.2)0.6.0
    6 0
      0
```

(10) 0.25

(3) 5	(7) 2	(11) 2.4
(4) 0.5	(8) 0.2	(12) 0.24

2

(1)
```
          3 0
1.2)3 6 0
    3 6
      0
```

(4)
```
        0.4
1.2)0.4.8
      4 8
        0
```

(7)
```
        0.6
1.4)0.8.4
      8 4
        0
```

(2)
```
          3
1.2)3.6
    3 6
      0
```

(5)
```
          6 0
1.4)8 4 0
    8 4
      0
```

(8)
```
        0.4
1.4)0.5.6
      5 6
        0
```

(3)
```
        0.3
1.2)0.3.6
      3 6 .
        0
```

(6)
```
          6
1.4)8.4
    8 4
      0
```

25 Division of Decimals — pp 50, 51

1

(1)
```
        1 5
1.4)2 1 0
    1 4
      7 0
      7 0
        0
```

(5) 24

(9) 32.5

(2)
```
        1.5
1.4)2.1.0
    1 4
      7 0
      7 0
        0
```

(6) 2.4

(10) 3.25

(3)
```
        0.1 5
1.4)0.2.1 0
      1 4
        7 0
        7 0
          0
```

(7) 0.24

(11) 0.325

(4) 0.25

(8) 0.16

(12) 0.525

2

(1) 80	(4) 0.6	(7) 0.4
(2) 8	(5) 40	(8) 0.9
(3) 0.8	(6) 4	

26 Division of Decimals — pp 52, 53

1

(1)
```
          1 3 0
1.9)2 4 7 0
    1 9
      5 7
      5 7
        0
```

(5) 270

(9)
```
          1 4 5
3.8)5 5 1 0
    3 8
      1 7 1
      1 5 2
        1 9 0
        1 9 0
            0
```

(2)
```
        1 3
1.9)2 4.7
    1 9
      5 7
      5 7
        0
```

(6) 27

(10)
```
          1 4.5
3.8)5 5.1
    3 8
      1 7 1
      1 5 2
        1 9 0
        1 9 0
            0
```

(3)
```
        1.3
1.9)2.4.7
    1 9
      5 7
      5 7
        0
```

(7) 2.7

(11)
```
          1.4 5
3.8)5.5.1
    3 8
      1 7 1
      1 5 2
        1 9 0
        1 9 0
            0
```

(4) 1.4

(8) 2.4

(12) 2.24

2

(1) 3.5	(5) 36	(9) 3.5
(2) 0.65	(6) 6.5	(10) 0.8
(3) 2.5	(7) 4.5	
(4) 0.06	(8) 1.6	

27 Division of Decimals — pp 54, 55

1

(1)
```
        4
1.2)4.8
    4 8
      0
```

(5)
```
        5
1.5)7.5
    7 5
      0
```

(9) 4

(2)
```
         4 0
0.12)4.8 0
     4 8
       0
```

(6)
```
         5 0
0.15)7.5 0
     7 5
       0
```

(10) 40

(3)
```
        4
0.12)0.4 8
     4 8
       0
```

(7)
```
        5
0.15)0.7 5
     7 5
       0
```

(11) 4

(4)
```
        4
0.13)0.5 2
     5 2
       0
```

(8)
```
        6
0.16)0.9 6
     9 6
       0
```

(12) 4

2

(1)
```
        3.5
1.6)5.6.0
    4 8
      8 0
      8 0
        0
```

(5) 7.5

(9) 8.5

(2)
```
        0.3 5
1.6)0.5.6 0
    4 8
      8 0
      8 0
        0
```

(6) 0.75

(10) 2.35

(3)
```
         3.5
0.16)0.5 6.0
     4 8
       8 0
       8 0
         0
```

(7) 7.5

(4)
```
         3.4
0.25)0.8 5.0
     7 5
     1 0 0
     1 0 0
         0
```

(8)
```
         2.4 5
2.4)5.8.8 0
    4 8
    1 0 8
      9 6
      1 2 0
      1 2 0
          0
```

28 Three Decimals ◆Mixed Calculations — pp 56, 57

1
(1) 2.24 (4) 7
(2) 1.28 (5) 0.72
(3) 1.26 (6) 2

2
(1) 12.3 (3) 12.88
(2) 0.6   (4) 2.4

3
(1) 7.4   (3) 2.6
(2) 1.8   (4) 4.2

4
(1) 7.8   (4) 2.8
(2) 2.1   (5) 35
(3) 4   (6) 0.9

29 Decimals Review — pp 58, 59

1
(1) 29.6   (5) 274.5 (9) 17.45   (13) 23.46
(2) 45.6   (6) 8.4   (10) 13.52
(3) 218   (7) 205.1 (11) 384.8
(4) 208.8 (8) 0.9   (12) 15.16

2
(1) 8.5   (5) 1.05   (9) 2.5
(2) 4.32   (6) 0.5   (10) 16.2
(3) 2.25   (7) 24   (11) 0.82
(4) 0.82   (8) 3.5   (12) 26

Advice
If you made many mistakes in **1**, start reviewing on page 12.
If you made many mistakes in **2**, start reviewing on page 32.

30 Fractions Review — pp 60, 61

1
(1) 1   (5) 1
(2) 1   (6) 2
(3) 2   (7) 1
(4) 2   (8) 2

2
(1) $1\frac{1}{2}$ (6) $1\frac{2}{7}$
(2) $1\frac{1}{3}$ (7) $2\frac{2}{3}$
(3) $1\frac{3}{4}$ (8) $1\frac{2}{9}$
(4) $1\frac{3}{5}$ (9) $2\frac{1}{2}$
(5) $1\frac{1}{6}$ (10) $2\frac{2}{5}$

3
(1) $1\frac{3}{5}$ (10) $1\frac{1}{4}$
(2) $1\frac{1}{7}$ (11) 1
(3) 1   (12) $1\frac{4}{9}$
(4) $1\frac{1}{9}$ (13) $1\frac{2}{3}$
(5) $1\frac{2}{11}$ (14) $1\frac{6}{7}$
(6) 2   (15) $1\frac{7}{8}$
(7) $2\frac{1}{3}$ (16) 1
(8) $1\frac{1}{8}$ (17) $1\frac{5}{9}$
(9) 1   (18) $1\frac{5}{7}$

1
(1) $1\frac{2}{5}$ (6) 1
(2) $2\frac{2}{3}$ (7) 2
(3) $1\frac{1}{4}$ (8) 1
(4) $1\frac{2}{7}$ (9) 2
(5) $1\frac{1}{9}$ (10) 2

2
(1) $\frac{7}{5}$ (6) $\frac{\boxed{3}}{3}$
(2) $\frac{8}{3}$ (7) $\frac{\boxed{6}}{3}$
(3) $\frac{5}{4}$ (8) $\frac{\boxed{4}}{4}$
(4) $\frac{9}{7}$ (9) $\frac{\boxed{10}}{5}$
(5) $\frac{10}{9}$ (10) $\frac{\boxed{14}}{7}$

3
(1) $\frac{3}{2}$ (11) $\frac{7}{4}$
(2) $\frac{5}{4}$ (12) $\frac{11}{4}$
(3) $\frac{7}{3}$ (13) $\frac{9}{5}$
(4) $\frac{5}{2}$ (14) $\frac{13}{9}$
(5) $\frac{7}{4}$ (15) $\frac{13}{11}$
(6) $\frac{7}{5}$ (16) $\frac{13}{7}$
(7) $\frac{8}{7}$ (17) $\frac{11}{5}$
(8) $\frac{11}{9}$ (18) $\frac{13}{6}$
(9) $\frac{11}{5}$ (19) $\frac{15}{11}$
(10) $\frac{8}{3}$ (20) $\frac{12}{7}$

1
(1) $1\frac{2}{3}$ (11) 1
(2) $1\frac{2}{7}$ (12) $2\frac{1}{3}$
(3) $1\frac{3}{5}$ (13) $2\frac{1}{2}$
(4) 2 (14) $1\frac{7}{9}$
(5) $1\frac{4}{9}$ (15) $1\frac{6}{7}$
(6) $1\frac{1}{8}$ (16) 2
(7) 2 (17) $1\frac{1}{4}$
(8) 2 (18) $2\frac{1}{5}$
(9) $1\frac{4}{11}$ (19) $1\frac{4}{7}$
(10) $1\frac{1}{6}$ (20) $1\frac{6}{11}$

2
(1) $\frac{\boxed{5}}{5}$ (5) $\frac{\boxed{18}}{9}$
(2) $\frac{\boxed{6}}{6}$ (6) $\frac{\boxed{8}}{8}$
(3) $\frac{\boxed{6}}{3}$ (7) $\frac{\boxed{7}}{7}$
(4) $\frac{\boxed{8}}{4}$ (8) $\frac{\boxed{14}}{7}$

3
(1) $\frac{7}{4}$ (7) $\frac{7}{3}$
(2) $\frac{8}{3}$ (8) $\frac{14}{9}$
(3) $\frac{9}{5}$ (9) $\frac{15}{8}$
(4) $\frac{13}{6}$ (10) $\frac{9}{4}$
(5) $\frac{3}{2}$ (11) $\frac{13}{7}$
(6) $\frac{11}{7}$ (12) $\frac{14}{11}$

Advice

If you scored over 85 on this section, review your mistakes
and move on to the next section.
If you scored between 75 and 84 on this section, begin
reviewing on page 60 before moving on.
If you scored less than 74 on this section, it might be a
good idea to go back to our "Grade 4 Decimals &
Fractions" book and do an extended review before
continuing.

1
(1) $\frac{4}{5}$ (6) $\frac{5}{7}+\frac{2}{7}=\frac{7}{7}=1$
(2) $\frac{2}{5}+\frac{3}{5}=\frac{\boxed{5}}{5}=\boxed{1}$ (7) $\frac{5}{9}$
(3) $\frac{4}{5}+\frac{1}{5}=\frac{5}{5}=1$ (8) $\frac{4}{9}+\frac{5}{9}=\frac{9}{9}=1$
(4) $\frac{6}{7}$ (9) $\frac{10}{11}$
(5) $\frac{3}{7}+\frac{4}{7}=\frac{7}{7}=1$ (10) $\frac{8}{11}+\frac{3}{11}=\frac{\boxed{11}}{11}=1$

2
(1) $\frac{3}{5}$ (6) 1
(2) 1 (7) $1\frac{1}{7}$
(3) $\frac{2}{5}+\frac{4}{5}=\frac{\boxed{6}}{5}=\boxed{1}\frac{\boxed{1}}{5}$ (8) $1\frac{2}{7}$
(4) $1\frac{2}{5}$ (9) 1
(5) $1\frac{1}{5}$ (10) $1\frac{2}{9}$

1
(1) $1\frac{3}{5}$ (6) $3\frac{2}{3}$
(2) $2\frac{4}{7}$ (7) $6\frac{2}{5}$
(3) $3\frac{5}{9}$ (8) $6\frac{1}{8}$
(4) $5\frac{2}{5}$ (9) $5\frac{7}{9}$
(5) $7\frac{3}{7}$ (10) $8\frac{1}{4}$

2
(1) $2\frac{3}{5}$ (6) $2\frac{5}{9}$
(2) $3\frac{4}{5}$ (7) $4\frac{7}{9}$
(3) $1\frac{5}{7}$ (8) $6\frac{8}{9}$
(4) $3\frac{5}{7}$ (9) $3\frac{9}{11}$
(5) $5\frac{6}{7}$ (10) $4\frac{9}{11}$

1
(1) $2\frac{2}{3}+\frac{2}{3}=2\frac{\boxed{4}}{3}=3\frac{1}{3}$ (6) $\frac{4}{5}+1\frac{2}{5}=1\frac{6}{5}=2\frac{1}{5}$
(2) $3\frac{4}{5}+\frac{3}{5}=3\frac{\boxed{7}}{5}=4\frac{2}{5}$ (7) $3\frac{4}{7}$
(3) $1\frac{4}{7}+\frac{5}{7}=1\frac{9}{7}=2\frac{2}{7}$ (8) $4\frac{5}{7}$
(4) $3\frac{2}{9}+\frac{8}{9}=3\frac{10}{9}=4\frac{1}{9}$ (9) $3\frac{2}{9}$
(5) $2\frac{5}{11}+\frac{9}{11}=2\frac{14}{11}=3\frac{3}{11}$ (10) $4\frac{4}{11}$

2
(1) $1\frac{2}{3}+2\frac{2}{3}=3\frac{\boxed{4}}{3}=4\frac{1}{3}$ (6) $4\frac{2}{5}$
(2) $1\frac{3}{5}+2\frac{3}{5}=3\frac{6}{5}=4\frac{1}{5}$ (7) $6\frac{3}{5}$
(3) $2\frac{3}{7}+3\frac{6}{7}=5\frac{9}{7}=6\frac{2}{7}$ (8) $5\frac{3}{7}$
(4) $3\frac{7}{9}+1\frac{7}{9}=4\frac{14}{9}=5\frac{5}{9}$ (9) $6\frac{1}{7}$
(5) $4\frac{7}{11}+2\frac{6}{11}=6\frac{13}{11}=7\frac{2}{11}$ (10) $6\frac{2}{9}$

36 Addition of Fractions pp72,73

1. (1) $2\frac{2}{3}+\frac{1}{3}=2\frac{\boxed{3}}{3}=\boxed{3}$ (6) 4
   (2) $3\frac{3}{5}+\frac{2}{5}=3\frac{\boxed{5}}{5}=4$ (7) 5
   (3) $3\frac{1}{5}+1\frac{4}{5}=4\frac{5}{5}=5$ (8) 3
   (4) $\frac{2}{7}+3\frac{5}{7}=3\frac{7}{7}=4$ (9) 5
   (5) $2\frac{2}{7}+1\frac{5}{7}=3\frac{7}{7}=4$ (10) 3

2. (1) $\frac{7}{9}$ (7) $5\frac{4}{5}$
   (2) $1\frac{3}{7}$ (8) $1\frac{1}{11}$
   (3) 1 (9) 1
   (4) $3\frac{2}{3}$ (10) $4\frac{3}{7}$
   (5) 3 (11) $5\frac{1}{9}$
   (6) $4\frac{1}{5}$ (12) 6

37 Subtraction of Fractions pp74,75

1. (1) $\frac{2}{5}$ (6) $\frac{3}{5}$
   (2) $\frac{3}{7}$ (7) $\frac{4}{7}$
   (3) $\frac{3}{7}$ (8) $\frac{5}{7}$
   (4) 0 (9) $\frac{5}{9}$
   (5) $\frac{5}{9}$ (10) $\frac{4}{9}$

2. (1) $\frac{2}{3}+\frac{1}{3}=\boxed{1}$ (4) $\frac{2}{5}+\frac{\boxed{3}}{5}=1$
   (2) $\frac{2}{3}+\frac{\boxed{1}}{3}=1$ (5) $\frac{2}{7}+\frac{\boxed{5}}{7}=1$
   (3) $\frac{3}{4}+\frac{\boxed{1}}{4}=1$ (6) $\frac{7}{9}+\frac{\boxed{2}}{9}=1$

3. (1) $\frac{1}{4}$ (4) $\frac{2}{9}$
   (2) $\frac{1}{3}$ (5) $\frac{5}{7}$
   (3) $\frac{5}{6}$ (6) $\frac{3}{5}$

38 Subtraction of Fractions pp76,77

1. (1) $2\frac{4}{5}-\frac{1}{5}=2\frac{\boxed{3}}{5}$ (6) $2\frac{6}{7}-2=\frac{6}{7}$
   (2) $3\frac{3}{5}-\frac{2}{5}=3\frac{1}{5}$ (7) $3\frac{4}{7}-\frac{4}{7}=3$
   (3) $2\frac{3}{5}-2=\frac{\boxed{3}}{\boxed{5}}$ (8) $3\frac{7}{9}-\frac{5}{9}=3\frac{2}{9}$
   (4) $2\frac{3}{5}-\frac{3}{5}=2$ (9) $2\frac{8}{9}-\frac{3}{9}=2\frac{5}{9}$
   (5) $3\frac{5}{7}-\frac{2}{7}=3\frac{3}{7}$ (10) $3\frac{5}{11}-3=\frac{5}{11}$

2

(1) $2\frac{3}{5}-1\frac{1}{5}=1\frac{\boxed{2}}{5}$ (6) $2\frac{5}{7}-1\frac{5}{7}=1$
(2) $2\frac{4}{5}-1\frac{3}{5}=1\frac{1}{5}$ (7) $3\frac{5}{9}-1\frac{1}{9}=2\frac{4}{9}$
(3) $\frac{2}{5}$ (8) $2\frac{5}{9}$
(4) $3\frac{4}{7}-1\frac{3}{7}=2\frac{1}{7}$ (9) $1\frac{1}{9}$
(5) $2\frac{2}{7}$ (10) $4\frac{8}{11}-1\frac{5}{11}=3\frac{3}{11}$

39 Subtraction of Fractions pp78,79

1. (1) $2-\frac{2}{5}=1\frac{\boxed{3}}{5}$ (6) $3\frac{4}{7}$
   (2) $1\frac{1}{5}$ (7) $4-\frac{3}{4}=3\frac{1}{4}$
   (3) $3-\frac{2}{7}=2\frac{5}{7}$ (8) $3\frac{4}{5}$
   (4) $2\frac{3}{7}$ (9) $2-\frac{2}{9}=1\frac{7}{9}$
   (5) $2\frac{1}{5}$ (10) $3\frac{7}{9}$

2. (1) $3-1\frac{2}{5}=1\frac{\boxed{3}}{5}$ (6) $3-1\frac{3}{7}=1\frac{4}{7}$
   (2) $4-1\frac{2}{5}=2\frac{3}{5}$ (7) $2\frac{2}{7}$
   (3) $3\frac{1}{5}$ (8) $1\frac{1}{7}$
   (4) $4\frac{4}{5}$ (9) $4-2\frac{5}{9}=1\frac{4}{9}$
   (5) $2\frac{2}{5}$ (10) $2\frac{7}{9}$

40 Subtraction of Fractions pp80,81

1. (1) $1\frac{\boxed{11}}{7}$ (6) $2\frac{\boxed{7}}{5}$
   (2) $1\frac{\boxed{12}}{7}$ (7) $3\frac{\boxed{9}}{5}$
   (3) $1\frac{\boxed{13}}{7}$ (8) $4\frac{\boxed{8}}{5}$
   (4) $2\frac{\boxed{11}}{7}$ (9) $4\frac{\boxed{9}}{5}$
   (5) $2\frac{\boxed{13}}{7}$ (10) $4\frac{\boxed{7}}{6}$

2. (1) $3\frac{1}{5}-\frac{4}{5}=2\frac{6}{5}-\frac{4}{5}=2\frac{\boxed{2}}{5}$ (6) $4\frac{1}{5}-\frac{3}{5}=3\frac{6}{5}-\frac{3}{5}=3\frac{3}{5}$
   (2) $3\frac{2}{7}-\frac{5}{7}=2\frac{\boxed{9}}{7}-\frac{5}{7}=2\frac{4}{7}$ (7) $4\frac{2}{5}-\frac{3}{5}=3\frac{7}{5}-\frac{3}{5}=3\frac{4}{5}$
   (3) $3\frac{3}{7}-\frac{5}{7}=2\frac{\boxed{10}}{7}-\frac{5}{7}=2\frac{5}{7}$ (8) $4\frac{1}{5}-\frac{2}{5}=3\frac{6}{5}-\frac{2}{5}=3\frac{4}{5}$
   (4) $3\frac{4}{7}-\frac{5}{7}=2\frac{11}{7}-\frac{5}{7}=2\frac{6}{7}$ (9) $5\frac{1}{5}-\frac{4}{5}=4\frac{6}{5}-\frac{4}{5}=4\frac{2}{5}$
   (5) $3\frac{3}{7}-\frac{6}{7}=2\frac{10}{7}-\frac{6}{7}=2\frac{4}{7}$ (10) $5\frac{2}{5}-\frac{4}{5}=4\frac{7}{5}-\frac{4}{5}=4\frac{3}{5}$

1 (1) $3\frac{2}{7}-1\frac{5}{7}=2\boxed{\frac{9}{7}}-1\frac{5}{7}$ (6) $2\frac{3}{7}$

$\qquad =1\frac{4}{7}$

(2) $4\frac{1}{5}-1\frac{2}{5}=3\frac{6}{5}-1\frac{2}{5}$ (7) $4\frac{3}{5}$

$\qquad =2\frac{4}{5}$

(3) $3\frac{1}{7}-1\frac{3}{7}=2\frac{8}{7}-1\frac{3}{7}$ (8) $5\frac{3}{8}-3\frac{6}{8}=4\frac{11}{8}-3\frac{6}{8}$

$\qquad =1\frac{5}{7}$ $\qquad\qquad\qquad =1\frac{5}{8}$

(4) $4\frac{3}{7}-1\frac{4}{7}=3\frac{10}{7}-1\frac{4}{7}$ (9) $1\frac{6}{7}$

$\qquad =2\frac{6}{7}$

(5) $4\frac{2}{7}-2\frac{4}{7}=3\frac{9}{7}-2\frac{4}{7}$ (10) $6\frac{2}{9}-3\frac{4}{9}=5\frac{11}{9}-3\frac{4}{9}$

$\qquad =1\frac{5}{7}$ $\qquad\qquad\qquad =2\frac{7}{9}$

2 (1) $\frac{2}{5}$ (7) $\frac{7}{8}$

(2) $\frac{4}{7}$ (8) $\frac{6}{11}$

(3) $\frac{8}{9}$ (9) $2\frac{4}{7}$

(4) $2\frac{3}{7}$ (10) $2\frac{4}{7}$

(5) $3\frac{1}{3}$ (11) $1\frac{2}{5}$

(6) $\frac{8}{9}$ (12) $2\frac{5}{9}$

42 **Three Fractions** ♦Mixed Calculations   pp 84, 85

1 (1) $\frac{2}{7}+\frac{1}{7}+\frac{3}{7}=\frac{6}{7}$ (5) $\frac{5}{7}$

(2) $\frac{3}{7}+\frac{2}{7}+\frac{5}{7}=\frac{10}{7}=1\frac{3}{7}$ (6) $\frac{4}{9}$

(3) $\frac{2}{9}+\frac{4}{9}+\frac{1}{9}=\frac{7}{9}$ (7) $\frac{3}{5}$

(4) $\frac{2}{9}+\frac{5}{9}+\frac{4}{9}=\frac{11}{9}=1\frac{2}{9}$ (8) $\frac{10}{11}$

2 (1) $\frac{2}{7}$ (6) 1

(2) $\frac{4}{9}$ (7) $\frac{4}{7}$

(3) $\frac{5}{11}$ (8) $\frac{3}{7}+\left(\frac{5}{7}-\frac{4}{7}\right)=\frac{3}{7}+\frac{\boxed{1}}{7}=\frac{4}{7}$

(4) $\frac{4}{5}+\frac{3}{5}-\frac{2}{5}=\frac{5}{5}=1$ (9) $\frac{1}{7}$

(5) $1\frac{1}{9}$ (10) $\frac{1}{7}$

1 (1) $\frac{6}{7}$ (7) 1 **2** (1) $\frac{1}{9}$ (8) $\frac{1}{6}$

(2) 1 (8) $1\frac{2}{11}$ (2) $\frac{4}{5}$ (9) $1\frac{3}{7}$

(3) $1\frac{1}{9}$ (9) $2\frac{5}{9}$ (3) $\frac{1}{3}$ (10) $\frac{4}{11}$

(4) $1\frac{5}{6}$ (10) $4\frac{1}{9}$ (4) $2\frac{2}{5}$ (11) $2\frac{2}{5}$

(5) $5\frac{4}{9}$ (11) $4\frac{2}{7}$ (5) $1\frac{5}{7}$ (12) $1\frac{5}{7}$

(6) $1\frac{4}{7}$ (12) 5 (6) $2\frac{2}{9}$ (13) $1\frac{7}{9}$

$\qquad\qquad\qquad\qquad\qquad$ (7) $1\frac{3}{7}$

Advice

If you made many mistakes in **1**, start reviewing on page 66.

If you made many mistakes in **2**, start reviewing on page 74.